Looking Back
Moving Forward

A MEMOIR OF HEALING AND TRANSFORMATION

KAREN A MACE

For my fellow missionaries from Ecuador days and all those who have spoken into my life over the years.

First published by Ultimate World Publishing 2021
Copyright © 2021 Karen Mace

ISBN

Paperback: 978-1-922714-01-5
Ebook: 978-1-922714-02-2

Karen Mace has asserted her rights under the Copyright, Designs and Patents Act 1988 to be identified as the author of this work. The information in this book is based on the author's experiences and opinions. The publisher specifically disclaims responsibility for any adverse consequences which may result from use of the information contained herein. Permission to use information has been sought by the author. Any breaches will be rectified in further editions of the book.

All rights reserved. No part of this publication may be reproduced, stored in or introduced into a retrieval system, or transmitted in any form, or by any means (electronic, mechanical, photocopying, recording or otherwise) without the prior written permission of the author. Any person who does any unauthorised act in relation to this publication may be liable to criminal prosecution and civil claims for damages. Enquiries should be made through the publisher.

Scripture quotations taken from the Amplified Bible, unless otherwise indicated. Copyright 1954, 1958, 1962, 1964, 1065, 1987 by The Lockman Foundation. Used by permission. (www.Lockman.org)

Cover design: Ultimate World Publishing
Layout and typesetting: Ultimate World Publishing
Editor: Denise Howe
Cover photo copyrights: MARIA NURINCE DOMINGGAS-Shutterstock.com

Ultimate World Publishing
Diamond Creek,
Victoria Australia 3089
www.writeabook.com.au

TESTIMONIALS

I love this book. I read it before and reading this updated version is like reading it through fresh eyes. So much wisdom, practical help, hope and testimony to God's desire and ability to heal all wounds, for all people. It is great read as a stand-alone but also as a companion to Karen's other book, *A Grief Revealed*.

This book should, however, come with a health warning: WARNING: this book will change your life, do not read unless you want healing and freedom.

As I reread this book, it called to mind an ancient prayer: "I pray that you, being rooted and established in love, may have power, together with all the Lord's holy people, to grasp how wide and long and high and deep is the love of Christ, and to know this love that surpasses all knowledge—that you may be filled to the measure of all the fullness of God. Now to him who is able to do immeasurably more than all we ask or imagine, according to his power that is at work within us, to him be the glory in the church and in Christ Jesus throughout all generations, for ever and ever! Amen."

Thank you, Karen, for allowing God to take you on a journey of healing so that you might be a conduit of his grace and healing for others.

Diane Hooley

Karen's handling of grief comes from a place of knowing: knowing herself, the broader complexities of grief from a psychological understanding, and through a desire to connect more meaningfully with her Maker. It follows that her writing is incandescent with insights that make Looking Back Moving Forward so much more than a memoir. It is a journey companion for those of us who have likewise screamed big questions at God in the midst of hardship. Using her own tragic story, she gently but firmly points the way home to His arms.

Claire van Ryn

Karen takes us on a journey through the dark corridors of fear, doubt, and rejection. Along the way she paints a mosaic with word pictures. The tragic loss of her two daughters propelled her into a journey of grief that few of us encounter. Traveling with her into this world she reveals the issues that beset many of us on the road of life. Karen's life experiences have prepared her in a unique way to be a help to others struggling with these issues. Yet, in the course of events that overtake her she finds hope that is stunning and authentic. There is a God in heaven, and He loves you with an unfailing, everlasting love, and that is where you find the peace that you search for and long for. Karen so beautifully brings us to the point of acceptance of the care of our loving Father.

Frank Mikell

When I started reading this book, I was totally amazed with the absolute honesty in which Karen shares about her journey through rejection, fear, shame, guilt and turning her back on God. I am not sure what I was expecting to read but not having known many of the things that she has experienced in her life I suppose some of it came as a complete surprise. At the same time, it has also been of great encouragement to me that no matter what place we find ourselves in, God is always with us. I liked Karen's quote early in the book – "You can't take fear as a travelling companion if you want to go on a journey with me. I don't travel with fear." – Holy Spirit. For me, this sums up the whole essence of Karen's book and the journey that she has been on, and still is on. It is so relevant for all of us to be reminded of this each and every day.

Glenda Allred

This is a book that must be read. It is not an easy read. Karen shares her story with soul-baring honesty-laying open her journey to present day. It has not been an easy journey. Deep pain has been her companion.

Karen trusts the reader with her story, sharing painful and deep memories of her early life—her fears and experience, her feelings and her vulnerabilities. She shares the rawness of abandonment that produced feelings of unworthiness. She asks the questions—Why? Why me?

The book is not written chronologically but as the title states - it is in looking back, understanding the past, making sense of what God was teaching and saying and doing throughout her life, that Karen has been able to move forward. This she has done with a positivity evident in her writing as she shares lessons learned and reflects on the greater plan of God through it all.

The book is well written and as I joined Karen on her journey of exploration and reflection, I found nuggets of truth and profound wisdom all along the way. I found myself pausing many times to reflect on these truths. There is so much in this book to contemplate. It should not be read quickly. It should not be rushed. The exercises at the end of each chapter make this book a useful guide to the pathway of grief. Karen states "grief is my thing". And through this book she guides the reader skillfully and compassionately along their own journey of looking back and moving forward.

Sheila Leech

What we experience in life is not only for our situation. It can become a powerful testimony that can be used by God to help others navigate their challenges and joys.

Because Karen was vulnerable in addressing her struggle with guilt, shame, fear and anger, Holy Spirit brought HIS truth into her circumstances, enabling her true identity in Christ to emerge.

Many aspects of Karen's journey brought Aha! light bulb moments as we pressed into freedom available for us, individually and in our marriage. This freedom is not exclusive. It is available for every one of us who believe, because of Christ in us, the hope of glory! Why do we believe and settle for mediocrity's lie, when Jesus' promise in John 10:10 is for abundant life?

We believe that you also, with a heart desiring to be healed, will be touched as you absorb Looking Back Moving Forward.

Bron and Rob Baker

CONTENTS

Testimonials	v
About this book	5
Early Days	7
Conquering Fear	11
The Love of a Father	23
Understanding Love	33
Freedom	45
Ecuador – Introduction to missionary life	55
Home Ministry Assignment and Back to Ecuador	65
Pain	77
Trust	89
Looking Back Moving Forward - Return to Ecuador	97
Grief	115
Afterword	121
Also By Karen	123
Acknowledgements	135
About the Author	137

Ileana and Sarah, November 1993
Although no longer with us you are always in my heart.

May the Son of God, who is already formed in you, grow in you, so that for you he will become immeasurable, and that in you he will become laughter, exultation, the fullness of joy which no one can take from you.

—Isaac of Stella

ABOUT THIS BOOK

This is an updated version of Healing Begins in the Heart. Much of it is unchanged except for some extra editing, but there are some changes, otherwise an updated version would not be necessary. When I finished the book in 2014, I was unwell. I didn't realise at the time, but I was heading for a period of emotional and psychological burnout that was to last for most of 2015. So, the book was published, and I did little to let people know it was available. Despite that, people bought the book, and I began to receive emails and Facebook messages telling me that the book had impacted various readers in ways that could only have been supernatural. To hear that something you have written has changed someone's life and given them hope, is beyond encouraging. When I wrote the book, it took a long time. I resisted because once I started, I realised that through the writing I had to face pain that I had been avoiding. As I did so, I became acquainted with grief, and, not knowing it well, thought I had done my grieving once the book was published. I hadn't. And, so, this book has a chapter about a particular aspect of grief—anniversary grief— that I came to know well over the years.

This is not an autobiography and does not take a linear approach to my life. As I began to write, Holy Spirit brought many things to mind, and I wrote as they came. The result is this book. I have been told that it could be confusing for those who like to have things in sequence, so I am suggesting you read this as Holy Spirit guides you. Each chapter could stand alone, although the chapters about our call to Ecuador, our life there, and the events that took place while we were there which turned our lives upside down, should be read chronologically. If you are prompted to pick up Looking Back Moving Forward, read until Holy Spirit says "Stop!" as that is something He will want you to take note of. The questions at the end of the chapters are meant to stimulate your thinking and, in conjunction with the promptings of Holy Spirit, I trust you will find them helpful.

EARLY DAYS

They found me under a gooseberry bush. That was the response from Grandma when I asked her where I came from. We lived in a mining town on the rugged west coast of Tasmania, and most of the males in the town worked at the Hercules mine. They shovelled the ore into lumbering rail carts that trundled down the mountain to the send-off where Grandpa worked. He was in charge of the huge Clydesdale horses that faithfully and dependably plodded back and forth, hauling the ore from cart to buckets that then carried it to Rosebery, a thriving mining town about five miles from Williamsford. Our little house was a mining company house, and gooseberry bushes grew all down one side, so I didn't doubt for a minute that my grandparents had found me there after the stork carefully selected that household for me. However, after trying to pick some of the fruit and ending up with nasty scratches, I was curious as to how they had extracted me from underneath the bush, without any of us being hurt by the seriously vicious thorns. Having accepted that the stork had delivered me to Grandma's house, it came as a shock when a lady arrived one day and told me she was my mother. I was about three years old then. I'm sure Mum visited before that time, but I don't remember her.

Looking Back Moving Forward

Mum and Dad met when they were both in the armed services, Mum in the navy and Dad in the army. Dad was a much-loved and pampered younger son of a fierce Scottish mother and an equally frightening Welsh father. From the little Mum and Dad told me of their marriage, it was doomed from the beginning. Both Mum and Dad were heavy drinkers, and, according to Dad, Mum would often go off with one of her brothers, who was an alcoholic, and arrive home drunk and aggressive. According to Mum, Dad spent a lot of time and money at the races, rarely picking a winner. It seems that from early days this became the pattern, with neither of them recognising how destructive their behaviour was.

Religion was a problem too. On Mum's side, everyone professed to be Irish Catholic, while on Dad's side the family held very strict Baptist beliefs. My paternal grandfather was a lay preacher who loved to preach hellfire and brimstone—so my dad told me. Dad told stories of life as a young boy living with a father who saw himself as representing God as he handed out severe punishment for what would be considered just being a boy. Grandpa Morgan, in Dad's eyes, represented God, and Dad did not want to have an ongoing relationship of any kind with someone he was always wary and afraid of. He continued to read the Bible until he left home because he had to, but his understanding of it came through the filter of his earthly father's treatment of him rather than through Holy Spirit revelation. Dad never forgot the punishment so frequently administered by his father in anger and, in Dad's mind, condoned and ordered by an equally angry God. I didn't consciously decide that what Dad told me about God was truth, but I can see that the fear of God's punishment and rejection was intense, and that, coupled with the fear of hell and purgatory, emotionally and spiritually crippled me for many years.

Dad's parents never accepted Mum; they tolerated her only because Dad was their favourite son. There was a complete distaste for anything Catholic, and only a year before Dad and Mum married, Dad's older sister had been ostracised by the family for marrying a Catholic man.

Early Days

Dad never saw her again, and her name was not to be mentioned within Grandpa Morgan's hearing. While Mum and Dad were still married, Auntie Audrey, Dad's younger sister, visited them often. Auntie Audrey made the mistake of falling in love with a Catholic man too, a match totally opposed by her family. Unable to go against her parents and devastated by their opposition, Auntie Audrey chose instead to take her own life. Mum arrived home one day to find her sister-in-law had used their gas oven to commit suicide.

In the face of such a tumultuous relationship, it's not surprising that by the time I was eighteen months old, and Kim was three and a half, Mum and Dad had decided that they no longer wanted to live with each other. Dad's version was that he arrived home one day to find a note saying Mum had left him and taken both Kim and me. Mum's version was that she couldn't put up with it anymore, so she decided to leave. She dropped me off with her parents who lived in Williamsford, an isolated mining town in Tasmania, and deposited my sister, Kim, with Mum's eldest sister, Auntie Monnie, in Gippsland, Victoria. I occasionally heard Grandma telling Mum she should never have separated us. I understand why she would say that now. Kim and I never really knew each other as sisters. We never had the opportunity to bond, and later, when we were brought together, Kim told me she hated me, that it wasn't fair I got to live with Grandma and Grandpa while she had to live with Auntie Monnie, who was very hard on her. And that set the tone of our relationship—it was too hard after all the time apart for us to feel sisterly towards each other. After dropping us off, Mum went off to do what she wanted to do. Occasionally, Mum dropped in, sometimes with her latest boyfriend, but rarely enough that it didn't disrupt my life too much.

Possibly because Mum was not a frequent visitor, I objected strongly to her taking over and telling me what to do when she did come to visit. One way of demonstrating my displeasure was to pretend to be dead one morning when Mum called me to get ready for school. I thought I was doing well until the first whack of the hairbrush on my unsuspecting bottom! I'm not sure what was the loudest—my shriek of outrage, the crack of the brush breaking against my backside, or Grandma yelling, "What do you think you're doing, Ann?" When Mum was gone on my return from school that day, I wasn't upset at all.

CONQUERING FEAR

> You can't take fear as a travelling companion if you want to go on a journey with me. I don't travel with fear.
> **—Holy Spirit**

As a child I was quite fearless; climbing trees, leaping off the very high front veranda at Grandma's place, traipsing through the bush around Williamsford, walking with other children to Montezuma Falls following the bush track from Williamsford—all this before I was five years old! But something happened that allowed fear to enter my life. After that time, fear had a firm grip on me so that for most of my life I was afraid of a lot of things.

If we are in a battle, it's important to know our enemy if we are to have any hope of defeating him. In the past few years, I've learned a lot about fear; I lived with it for most of my life and am very aware of how it works. When we live with something for long enough, we become accustomed to it and begin to accept that it is normal. A big part of my work these days is to teach people to use writing to work through challenging or difficult life events. Where clients are receptive to it, I also use writing as a therapy in any counselling I do. It was while preparing for a therapeutic writing workshop that I decided to use a clustering exercise (a little like mind mapping), and needed a stimulus word, a feeling word. I chose fear—not with any particular motive in mind, but because many people seem to have a problem with fear. As I tried the exercise, I had an astonishing aha moment when the word rat popped into my mind. Immediately, I was back in a dark little bedroom in Grandma's house in Williamsford. Even at four, I was used to the dark as my bedroom was in the middle of the house, and once the lights were out, that was it. And I did not have a lamp in my room. I was just going off to sleep when I felt something run over the blankets covering my feet. My eyes popped open, my heart pounded a little, and then something else ran across my feet! I screamed, and almost immediately the door burst open, and the light came on. I saw the rat shoot out the door, but that wasn't what scared me. I was a little girl, afraid and needing hugs and reassurance. Instead, Mum shouted, "What the hell is wrong with you? Just go to sleep!" The fierceness of the words and the anger on Mum's face caused me to yank up the sheet and burrow into my bed. The light went out, and the door banged shut. That incident was over, but it left me with a sometimes-debilitating fear, a fear that, I learned many years later, came from Mum's words and her expression.

I was six when Mum decided it was time for me to go and live with her and John, the man we thought was her new husband. I left Grandma's house to live with them in New Norfolk, a small town in the south of Tasmania—a long way from Williamsford. St. Brigid's Convent was only a few minutes from the flat we lived in. I had attended St. Joseph's Convent School in Rosebery for a while before leaving Williamsford, but it was at St. Brigid's that religion became very important to me. I learned the catechism, and I knew what I could and couldn't do—what was a venial sin and what was a mortal sin—so I made sure I only committed venial sins. Unlike the mortal sins, which were a ticket straight to hell if you died before confessing them, venial sins would mean only a little more time in purgatory.

Conquering Fear

Just to be sure I was safe, I attended confession once a week at least, and I tried very hard to remember every single thing I had done so that I could start the next week with a clean slate. I loved words and performing and often played the part of one of the saints in our school plays. As St. Maria Goretti I did a spectacular faint, falling flat on my back on the hard wooden floor of the classroom, much to the enjoyment of my fellow grade three students. Sister Mary Alacoque was our teacher, and I remember how kind she was to me. I wanted to please her and attempted to learn everything I could about my religion, deciding to do my best because I wanted to be a nun, just like her. Surely if I became a nun God would be pleased with me.

One Friday afternoon when I was about twelve years old, I was at the swimming pool, and because I was hungry, I bought a pie, forgetting that it was Friday. I was halfway through the pie, thoroughly enjoying it, when a friend not so kindly reminded me that it was Friday. I was disappointed that I would have to throw away half the pie, but hot on the heels of disappointment came condemnation followed by an icy fear. It was only Friday afternoon, and confession wasn't until Saturday evening. I began imagining all sorts of disastrous scenarios—being hit by a car on the way home or being stung by a bee and dying from an allergic reaction (I had never been allergic to bees!), choking to death when I ate dinner that night and so on. Such ridiculous things were racing through my head, and I was allowing them not only to remain but to get bigger and bigger so that they became giants I could not defeat. What a difference it would have made if I had known then I could take captive the thoughts that were running riot (2 Corinthians 10:5), that I could think about my thinking. And how much anxiety and distress it would have saved if I had known that I have constant access to the Father through what Jesus has done. There were many wasted years of worrying and trying to make sure I kept to all the rules, always fearful that I would commit a sin and not know it, constantly afraid that when I died, God would turn me away from heaven because I had no right to be there. From the time I was very young,

I had a sense of being watched by God, but not in a loving, caring way; I was sure He was watching and condemning me, disdainful of me because I didn't measure up. And once Grandpa died, I believed he was watching me too, and always with a critical eye. It was easy for fear to control me, because I didn't read the Word and so did not know that verses like the following were in the Bible and were there for me: "And therefore the Lord earnestly waits expecting, looking and longing to be gracious to you; and therefore he lifts Himself up, that He may have mercy on you and show loving kindness to you. For the Lord is a God of justice. Blessed, happy, fortunate, to be envied are all those who earnestly wait for Him, who expect, and look and long for Him [for His victory, favour, His love, His peace, His joy, and His matchless, unbroken companionship]!" (Isaiah 30:18).

As a young girl living with mum and her partner, I often had to referee. Payday in the town we lived in was the busiest part of a fortnight for the local pubs. Sometimes Mum would go to the pub with everyone else, but more often than not, she would drink at home while John drank at the pub. I never quite knew what to expect, but inevitably, it meant little sleep, as there was a lot of aggression between the two of them and I usually attempted to intervene to keep them from doing actual harm to each other. We had a stainless-steel Hecla kettle; one night before I could stop her, Mum picked it up and hit John over the head with it. Every time I looked at the kettle after that, I vowed I would never be like Mum, and I would never have a relationship where violence and arguing were a part of it. The determination to avoid anything that might lead to the ugliness I saw while growing up, influenced how I related to my husband; when Ross and I even looked like disagreeing about something, let alone arguing, I would back away from it, not realising that I was responding to that vow I had made years before. Fear is the basis of low self-esteem, and it was low self-esteem that drove my thoughts about my inferiority to Ross. Despite being welcomed into the family, I knew I wasn't the sort of girl his parents would have chosen for him. I was definitely from the wrong side of the tracks. My concern about this and the toxic thoughts I allowed to go around and around in my mind, fed the belief that I was not good enough—not good enough for Ross, not good enough for his family, and not good enough for God. The result was that I resented having to spend too much time with the family. Family days, where everyone got together for some reason or another were frequent, and I found myself at times, although not always, becoming tense and angry. I realise now I was always concerned that I wouldn't measure up, that something about me would draw criticism. Although that didn't happen, my alarm centre, the amygdala, the part of the brain that is alert to any threat, was always on alert, because fear, that underlies low self-esteem, was ever present. Consequently, I was always ready for fight or flight, and I seemed to choose the fight.

Growing up, Catholicism defined, to some degree, how we acted, and there was a strong sense of being superior in that we believed the Catholic Church was the only true church. That's what we were taught, and we had no reason not to believe it. Yet, despite this, there was no relationship with God; our family was religious and adhered to the rules that, we hoped, would keep us from an eternity in hell. I was determined from a very young age to do everything possible to make sure I went to heaven and had the minimum time in purgatory on the way. I went to Mass not only on Sundays but through the week as well. I attended the Novena on the first Saturday of each month because I believed that was a sure way of getting to heaven. I said the Rosary diligently but never read the Bible as, in those days, lay people were not allowed to read the Bible for themselves. Mum bought a very large red leather-covered Bible, which sat on the bookshelf, and occasionally I was allowed to leaf through it because it was such a lovely book, but it was just a book. The only thing I recall in those early years that could be considered teaching was the Catechism we learned at school.

In the couple of years before we went to Bible College, we had good teaching through the Ravenswood Gospel Chapel where we attended church, but I see now that I had so much wrong teaching that I don't think there was room for much else to go in. Childhood experiences and relationships set the scene for our adult relationships, and much of what I needed to have cleaned out of me had made its home there from early days. Fear, for me, became a way of responding and relating, beginning with the experience with my mum when I was only four. Although I detested the constant anxiety and the feeling of a malevolent presence that dogged me, I didn't know what to do about it, so I just learned to live with fear. It controlled a lot of what I did—or didn't do. One day, still early in my Christian walk, I was sitting by the heater in our home in Ravenswood, Tasmania; our daughters, Miriam, then four, and Sarah, her younger sister, were playing quietly together for a change and I decided to read my Bible. As I opened it, fear overcame me; it was like a heavy weight pressing in on me, and with that oppression came a strong sense of danger. I just knew that if I continued reading, something terrible would happen to my children; I put the Bible down. I knew nothing about the battle I was in, and so I had no weapons. At that time, I wasn't aware of what God's Word says: "For though we walk in the flesh, we are not carrying on our warfare according to the flesh and using mere human weapons. For the weapons of our warfare are not physical weapons of flesh and blood, but they are mighty before God for the overthrow and destruction of strongholds" (2 Corinthians 10:3-4).

Because of this—because I didn't have a clue that Jesus had already set me free—fear influenced everything I did. Once fear came to stay, I was never very adventurous; I developed a fear of heights, I was always afraid of the dark, and I was afraid of what people might think of me and so became a people pleaser. I was afraid of not measuring up to others' expectations, afraid of failing—afraid of everything. To hide this, I wore an invisible mask. Often when I was afraid or uncertain, when I felt out of control, I used anger to cover the fear. Anger drives a wedge between people and destroys relationships. At the very least, relationships suffer, and I knew this anger was affecting my relationship with my children and my husband.

Now, today, I am excited to read how much God cares for me and am confident that the Word is true, and God does love me, I didn't know this back in the days when Ross and I were young parents and young in our relationship. I allowed fear to dictate how I responded, and I was open to the negative and totally unreasonable thoughts that came into my head. I did not know I could choose what to keep and what to throw out, and because I had very poor role models of what a good relationship might look like, I always expected the worst. We humans have a negativity bias. I believe God created us this way so that we quickly notice and thus avoid danger. However, sad to say, because of this, we tend to choose things based on our need to avoid negative experiences, and this can wreak havoc in a relationship. For Ross and me the negativity bias took a particular form: whenever something happened that we really should have discussed, I wouldn't talk about it, because I was afraid Ross might become angry, and if that happened, he might tell me to leave or he might leave. And Ross wasn't able to talk about things either. So we just pretended everything was OK when in reality things just built up because nothing was ever resolved. Insecurity was closely associated with fear, and so was low self-esteem; a sense of not being good enough was my constant companion.

When God called us to Ecuador, I was excited at first; but as the time drew nearer, fear crept in again. It started whispering in my ear, and soon uncertainty and feeling uncomfortable about going replaced anticipation. It was during this time that I had a dream. In the dream, we had landed at an airport that seemed to be in the middle of a city. Our plane was the only one on the runway, and there was a light fog surrounding us as we exited the plane to walked towards the airport building; I felt very much alone, and then I heard a voice say, "But I am with you." I knew it was God and felt a peace after that about going. I was to remember this dream later when Illy and Sarah died and wonder if I had really heard God at all.

In the year that God called us to be missionaries, my grandmother died. I loved Grandma. She took me in when Mum decided she wanted to go off and do her own thing, and I knew Grandma loved me. She wasn't very demonstrative, but each night after my bath, she sat me on her knee and we would have some time there in front of the fire, where Grandma would rock me and tell me a story as she held me safely in her arms. I remember her as a very special person.

After Grandma died, for some reason, I experienced spiritual attack like I had never known. It was frightening to be woken at two in the morning by the physical sensation of a slap across the face and an overwhelming sense of malevolence in the room. I had always had a deep, almost paralysing, fear of Satan but, despite this, I managed to wake Ross. Once awake, he felt the presence too, and we prayed; actually, we sang "In the Name of Jesus." We sang it over and over until we felt the presence leave. When this happened, we also felt the need to pray for protection for our girls in the next room, and I remember having a picture in my spirit of a huge dove hovering over them. I knew this meant that they were protected, and so we just proceeded to deal with the malevolent presence. It was exhausting, as this went on for about a week.

One evening, not long after the early morning battles faded, we were at the Riverside Presbyterian Church. Petros, Ross's band, was playing there. During the service, I began to feel very uncomfortable, and the impression that we needed to handle what had been happening was strong. I knew that when we got home, something was going to happen. I didn't want to do this and tried to shake off the feeling I had, but it wouldn't leave.

Once home with the girls settled, I told Ross what had happened during church, and we agreed that something had to be done but we weren't sure what; we called Tom and June, our pastors, who lived just down the road from us, and they came up. I knew fear didn't want this to happen, and I was so tempted to call it off, but June was used to dealing with these situations and we began to talk. We tried to understand where the attacks were coming from and since we had heard there was a coven in Ravenswood, one that was actively working against the Christian influence in that place, we thought it may have been from them. However, as we talked, it became clear that much of what was happening was related to my background, that there were many demonic influences in my life and they were present because of things that had happened in the past, including the choices I had made. As June began naming these spirits, a voice spoke that wasn't mine saying, "Once a Catholic, always a Catholic. You won't get rid of me." I remembered Mum saying that to me once after Ross and I met and began going to the Salvation Army, so it had obviously remained with me. My hands contorted as June prayed, and there was a serious battle going on. We were there for over three hours, and many demons were cast out, including fear—in the end June told the 'Legion' to go!

We were exhausted. But it was great to be free of those evil things. I had no idea that I had been carrying them around with me. God has perfect timing. Before this, I would have run a mile if there had been even a hint of anything supernatural happening.

Even though you decide to get rid of something, it will always come back if you don't have the right barriers in place to prevent it doing so, and not understanding how to keep a victory means that you will surely lose it—and I did. I didn't know how to keep a victory, so I also didn't know what barriers to use to prevent fear coming back. I was like the man Jesus speaks of in Matthew 12:43-45; "But when the unclean spirit has gone out of a man, it roams through dry [arid] places in search of rest, but it does not find any. Then it says, I will go back from which I came out. And when it arrives it finds the place unoccupied, swept, put in order, and decorated. Then it goes and brings with it seven other spirits more wicked than itself, and they go in and make their home there. And the last condition of that man becomes worse than the first."

Once we choose to live in relationship with God, fear can only keep us prisoner while we allow it to. It certainly stops us living a kingdom life of righteousness, peace, and joy in the Holy Spirit (Romans 14:17). Just a few years ago, Holy Spirit told me that it's not possible to go on a journey with Him if we take fear as a travelling companion. Those words remain with me although at the time they weren't specifically for me but for someone else who struggles with fear. They are words that apply to all of us who love God and are called by Him, and I have shared them with many Christians since that day. God clearly tells us in His Word that he has not given us a spirit of fear. I like the way the Amplified version says it: "For God did not give us a spirit of timidity (of cowardice, of craven and cringing and fawning fear), but [He has given us a spirit] of power and of love and a calm and well-balanced mind and discipline and self-control" (2 Timothy 1:7).

God encouraged me, through a dream, to trust Him with our lives in Ecuador, but I did not understand what that meant. I was still bound up in religion, and this—rather than relationship, rather than a "spirit of power and of love"—was what dictated how I lived.

Graham Cooke, in *Manifesting Your Spirit*, says that too many Christians have no frame of reference for God, no internal, personalised expression of God's presence. That's how I was, and the result was that I was tossed around from one fear to the next because I had no anchor, nothing to stabilise me. Despite the deliverance from oppressing spirits and despite being at Bible College, I didn't understand what it meant to live in relationship with God. I didn't know what it was to be filled with the Holy Spirit, to be empowered, so I was always trying to measure up, to do the right thing, to make people think well of me, to prove that I was good enough. Although I heard and read, many times, the verse, "Cease striving and know that I am God" (Psalm 46:10), I kept trying. And the harder I tried, the more elusive this goodness seemed. I had a strong conviction that I would never measure up and was desperately afraid that I would be eternally lost. The thoughts that plagued me of being turned away from heaven and being told by God that I wasn't worthy reflected this toxic thinking.

Conquering Fear

Fear seemed to have won. Timothy Jennings, in his book *The God-Shaped Brain*, talks about the Law of Liberty, which says that for love to exist, there needs to be freedom. Paul, in the second book of Corinthians 3:17 says it beautifully: "Now the Lord is the Spirit, and where the Spirit of the Lord is, there is liberty (emancipation from bondage, freedom)." When liberty is violated, there are consequences, and one of those is that love is damaged and may eventually be destroyed. Religion violates liberty. Fear gains control, and although initially there is a desire to rebel, when we surrender to the violations for long enough, we lose all sense of who we are—our individuality. We believe the lies that fear brings against us, not realising that the enemy is at work doing what he does—stealing, killing, and destroying. One of the principal ways he does this is by building strongholds that set themselves up against true knowledge of God (2 Cor. 10: 2-5). I was at war with what was setting itself up against true knowledge of God—who He is, what He is like—but hadn't a clue how to fight. I constantly asked, "Can I trust Him?" Satan lies about God and lies break the circle of love and trust. They violate liberty, and love cannot exist in that place. I had yet to learn that "perfect love casts out all fear." Perfect love reveals lies for what they are so that trust is restored, and love can flow. The perfect love I needed to understand was the love of Father God.

Try this:

Write about something that was significant to you in this chapter. What was it? Why was it significant? How will knowing it make a difference?

Set a timer for 5 minutes and write about what perfect love means to you. Begin with, Perfect love …

THE LOVE OF A FATHER

I have loved you with an everlasting love; therefore I have continued my faithfulness to you.
— **Jeremiah 31:3**

God pursues us. He desires a love relationship with us. Until we understand that, and can accept His love, everything we do is out of duty, a sense of obligation. Or maybe we do all we can to please Him in the hope He will then say we've done enough to get to heaven.

James (pseudonym) is a solid Christian who goes to church regularly, is involved in several church programs, and is also an Elder. In a conversation where eternity became the focus, James commented that he "hoped he had done enough to secure himself a place." While he said it in a partly joking manner, when I spoke to him later, he confirmed that he had no confidence that God accepted him and loved him, and he said, *"loving God is just too hard when I am so afraid of Him."* James is not the only one I have heard say such things. Many Christians are busy trying to please God because they can't accept that nothing we do can change how God loves us. Jesus has done all that is necessary to reconcile us to God, but even before the Cross, God loved us so much

He was willing to sacrifice His only Son to make reconciliation possible. Nothing we can do will make God love us more—or love us less.

Charles Blackaby, in *Experiencing God*, says that if we don't live our lives out of the overflow of God's love for us and our love for Him, then we can't live the Christian life as it is intended. Distance characterised my life for a long time, just as it characterised my relationship with my earthly father. Many years after Mum and Dad divorced, Mum told me she had married Dad because she wanted two children. I believed her because she left Dad not long after she had her two daughters. I suppose I was fortunate that Mum left me with my grandparents. My sister, Kim, always said she loved Auntie Monnie, but spoke with intense bitterness about the beatings and the very strict discipline that was so much a part of her upbringing. The resentment she felt seemed to settle on me; after all, in Kim's eyes, I had a much easier time of it with Grandma and Grandpa.

Dad figured little in our lives. He was faithful, Grandma said, in sending monetary support for me, and he always sent gifts for birthday and Christmas. Occasionally we went to Melbourne to visit aunts who lived there, and I'd have some time with Dad then. He was always kind to me and took me to see his family, who are nothing but shadowy figures in my memories. Grandma Morgan was always in black, in a darkened room at the back of the corner store they owned. Uncle Max always gave me lollies.

I don't remember Grandpa Morgan. He was a hard man, a lay Baptist preacher who spoke forcefully of hell, drawing such frightening pictures of it that Dad was afraid of doing anything wrong for a very long time. Punishment was quick if Dad stepped outside Grandpa's understanding of how a Christian should act. Dad knew the Bible and could quote any verse. He had to learn several verses each week as a child and was severely punished in God's name if he didn't manage the required number of verses.

When only ten years old, Dad decided he would like to stay home from an evening service. The services went for a long time and Dad said he hadn't been well and wanted to go to bed early to be ready for school the next day. The day was sultry. Dark clouds rolled in towards the city, thunder rumbled in the distance, and lightning lit up the gloomy dark sky. Just to the left of the back door was a rain barrel already three-quarters full from recent downpours. Grandpa's anger was almost palpable as he reached out and grabbed Dad by the shirt collar. Shaking and dragging Dad, Grandpa yelled at Uncle Max to open the back door. He then lifted Dad off the floor and dumped him into the rain barrel. Dad was petrified but knew that anything he said would only enrage Grandpa more. *"You will stay in that rain barrel until we return from service. While you are there you repent of your sins and pray that God will forgive you."* As dad recounted the story, he repeated Grandpa's words with such bitterness I knew the memory still hurt. From that day, Dad told me, he wanted nothing more to do with a God who was so angry.

Dad's example of being a father grew out of his own experience of being fathered. His father's harsh interpretation of the Scriptures warped Dad's experience, which translated into an angry, cold, and distant relationship that Dad could never understand, nor embrace. He decided that it was safer to ignore God—safer for him, because he never wanted to come under that punitive control again. Duty was important though, and Dad always did his duty towards us. He provided for us financially but having never had a loving relationship with his own father meant he didn't know how to do that with his daughters. So distance was the safe way.

I didn't understand all the above when I was young. Seeing God as father wasn't a good thing for me. I was wary of Him. I had a couple of role models, one of them being my father, who in my eyes had abandoned me. I always felt that I wasn't good enough for him; that somehow it was my fault he didn't want me. So how on earth could I be good enough for God, who was far above and beyond all I could imagine a father might be?

Another father model I had was Grandpa. I love him for the attempts he made to connect with a young child whose parents didn't want her. Most Saturdays he would go to Rosebery, to the pub, where he would drink and bet on the horses. Every time he went, he brought back a small bag of spearmint logs for me. Mostly, he was distant, and I learned not to be a nuisance, but I have fond memories of sitting on the old wood horse with him shelling peas for Sunday lunch. I remember one night when Mum was visiting and was to babysit while Grandma visited with the neighbours. I suppose Mum thought I was safe in bed and asleep when she and her boyfriend decided to go to the pub. All might have been well if a ferocious storm hadn't come up. Thunder so loud and powerful it shook the house and rattled the crockery on the sideboard woke me and caused me to leap from my bed intending to hop in with Grandma. My bedroom door opened onto a hallway lit by a small lamp, but the sizzling crackle that came as I stepped into the hall must have been lightning striking a transformer. One minute I was standing in the safety of a familiar place, and the next the darkness was so profound I felt totally disorientated. My fear-filled scream woke Grandpa, whose room backed onto mine. He was there in an instant, the thumping and muttering as he came reassuring enough that my pounding heart started to calm.

The rough *"What's wrong with you girl?"* was quickly followed by *"Where's your mother?"* Without waiting for a reply, and muttering words I probably wasn't supposed to hear, Grandpa picked me up—how he could see, I do not know—and carried me back to his room. I'll never forget how he let me hop in his bed while he sat in a chair and waited for Grandma to come home.

Although I knew Grandpa loved me in his own way, I somehow understood I couldn't rely on him. Just like Dad, Grandpa didn't know how to love. I saw how he was with Grandma—it was an uneasy union. And I knew that when he was in one of his silent moods nothing would make him talk; it was better to leave him until he got over whatever it was he was stewing about. Sometimes he would go bush for days, all alone, because he didn't want anyone's company but his own. One time his silence lasted for three months.

John, I suppose, was the other father model I had. When I was five, I was told Mum had married again, although when I was seventeen, I found that she never had married but had a de facto relationship with John, although he wanted them to marry. John was fourteen years younger than Mum, and this led to all sorts of interesting dynamics in their relationship. I was only six when Mum took me from Grandma's to live with her and John in New Norfolk, a town in the south of Tasmania that was well known for its high rate of teen pregnancies, alcoholism, and broken marriages. Most people worked either at the pulp and paper mill or the state's infamous mental institution located in town. Mum was a psychiatric nurse and initially worked at the main mental institution but later moved to another that was for elderly folk with psychiatric conditions.

I don't know when the rage started but I became an angry child. Mum and John frequently left me alone while they worked, and I learned quickly to take care of myself. I looked back on my time with Grandma and Grandpa and longed to go back to what I remembered as a safe place. One afternoon, alone again, the longing for Grandma was so strong, I decided to walk back to Williamsford! I packed up my doll, let myself out, and started on the long walk home. Over the bridge I went and out along the road I knew led to Queenstown. Needless to say, I didn't get far. A friend of Mum recognised me and reported my escape to her.

Increasingly, I could recognise when Mum had been drinking, although she hid it well for many years. I think my anger with her grew with the knowledge of her frailties. By the time I was a teenager, I was frequently angry with Mum. I didn't know any other way to express my frustration. I hated the way Mum and John fought, the way she drew me and my sister, who came to live with us when I was eight, into the games she played. I hated that Mum was drinking so much, and most of all, I hated that I couldn't trust her. The only way

I knew to let her know how I felt was to rebel. At every turn I fought and argued, and when anger became fury I threw things, making life difficult for Mum until she gave in and let me have, or do, whatever it was we were arguing about. I was also angry with John. I saw him as weak, and I did my best to avoid him.

There was no warmth in our home, no sense of it being a safe place. With things the way they were between Mum and John, it was no wonder I dreaded those nights around payday. Perhaps because of the alcohol, Mum and John's relationship had deteriorated to the place where they rarely communicated with each other until Mum wanted something from him. As soon as she had it, the distance was there again and frequently so was the silent treatment, just like Grandpa's. Often, this silence would extend to Kim and me as well, so that there was a sense of dread hanging over the house; we walked on eggshells, never knowing what the right thing to do was, afraid of aggravating the already shaky situation. Payday always equated to drunkenness. John stayed out late and rolled in, barely able to walk, while Mum had her sherry delivered by the local taxi. My sister and I shared a bedroom with no lock on the door. I can't remember when I started closing the door at night; I just know that a time came when I wanted to put up a barrier in an attempt to keep out what I sensed wanted to harm me. My sister slept through everything, or pretended to, but I lay awake, heart pounding so I could hear it in my ears, facing away from the door furiously saying Hail Marys, hoping that tonight there wouldn't be a presence by my bed, one that seemed to stand there forever before turning and leaving. Perhaps it was my perception of threat, but I felt very vulnerable. I couldn't rely on Mum to protect me, as she usually drank to oblivion so that nothing would wake her, or was on a night shift and not even there. I tried putting a knife in the door to act as a lock, but the door opened so forcefully the knife bent almost in half. In those days, Mum worked a night shift from 8.00 p.m.- 8.00 a.m. Although no one ever said why, once my sister

The Love of a Father

left home, Mum took me with her when she worked the night shift and I slept in one of the empty beds.

I saw God through Grandpa and Dad, and, to some extent, through John too. Dad abandoned and rejected me, Grandpa loved me in an off-hand, don't-get-in-my-way manner; and John had no idea what to do with me. I think they all saw me through a duty lens.

Although wary and afraid of God, I wanted Him to accept me because I didn't want to go to hell or spend an extended period in purgatory. I worked hard to accumulate points with God. I went to Mass every week and often on weekday mornings too. I made sure I went to confession regularly and attended the Novena on the first Saturday of every month. I was determined that God wouldn't be able to say I didn't come up to the mark. Yet, I knew it was never enough. I felt with God as I did when Mum was drunk, and she and John weren't on speaking terms—as though I were walking on eggshells. I even thought that God was like my paternal grandfather who used the Bible, God's Word, as an instrument of punishment and control. Having never read the Bible, I had no idea what it said and did not know it could be living, and powerful, and full of revelation about how much God loves us.

A few years after I became a Christian, Sue (pseudonym), a nurse, and I were working together one evening as we often did. We had a lady in isolation who was being specialled (that is she needed one-on-one attention from a nurse) and before I could ask where she wanted to work, Sue offered to spend the evening with that patient. I knew she didn't enjoy working in the isolation wards, so I assured her I would be happy to go in. *"No,"* she said firmly. *"I need to do this. I hope this will get me into God's good books; earn me a few points, I've been a bit slack lately."* I was a bit taken aback, but as I reflect on that time, I didn't respond to her except to shrug and agree that she should do whatever she felt she needed to. Having grown up in the Catholic faith with an emphasis on accumulating credit to get to heaven without going through purgatory, I understood her thinking, although hearing someone actually say what I had believed for many years made me pause for a minute. Now when I think about it, I understand that I wasn't sure myself, so I had nothing to offer Sue as far as reassuring her that she didn't need to work for God's approval by doing things. In fact, in my own way, I was still working hard to gain God's approval. We can serve God, worship Him, believe in Him, and fear Him without loving Him and living a loving relationship with Him.

I lived many years treading gingerly, waiting for the axe to fall. It meant I was weak, vulnerable, and very susceptible to Satan's lies and the deception he is so effective at weaving. That he comes to steal, kill, and destroy is very true (John 10:10), and it is so much easier for him when we have no idea how much God loves us, and no real understanding of what Jesus has done for us—no idea of who we really are in Christ. That was me.

I first heard of the word *hesed* when reading *The Gospel According to Job* by Mike Mason, a book given to me by a friend, Susan Olsen, a few months after Illy and Sarah died. Understanding how overwhelming life was at the time, Susan suggested I put the book aside until I felt ready to read it. Hesed is an incredibly beautiful Hebrew word found twice in the book of Job. Mason says it is so rich in meaning it is almost untranslatable and the best we can do is the Anglo-Saxon word *love*. The word carries the meaning of the love of Father God—consistent, ever-faithful, relentless, constantly pursuing, lavish, extravagant, and unrestrained. We sometimes see it translated "loving kindness" or "steadfast love." Why do so many of us struggle as we do with the word love? When I read 1 Corinthians 13, I wonder if it is ever possible to love that way. I remember when we were newly married, I was shocked that Ross could speak to me the way he did one day when I left the car window down a fraction. How could he love me and still speak so rudely to me? But both of us have come a long way since that day, and the God of *hesed* has become so much more a part of our lives that as we grow in His love, we see that love at work in us too. How

The Love of a Father

we relate to each other is much more a demonstration of love than it ever was in those early days.

We throw that word, love, around a lot. We hear it from the lips of pop stars who want their fans to know their appreciation, we hear it from parents to children, and vice versa in a throwaway manner as they all run from one thing to another, and we hear it from those who use it to manipulate and get what they want at the expense of anyone who might get in their way. When life is good, and things are going the way we want them to, it's easy to say, "Yes, I love God, you, everyone." I know because I did … until my mother died while I was thousands of miles away, my daughters died while we were serving God as missionaries in a country far from home, and our only remaining daughter threw in our faces everything we wanted for her and told us she was pregnant and was going to marry the father—at sixteen.

Mike Mason says in *The Gospel According to Job*, that if we are getting our own way and things are going as we want them to, love sits well with us and the word rolls fluently off our tongues, while for those who are suffering, it becomes a word to hate intensely. That made sense to me. You begin to steer away from that word, to cringe inside when you hear it, and cynicism grows as you hear those who suffering hasn't touched talking about how much God loves you. The pain becomes a filter that everything you hear must pass through and because of its very nature, pain is not a very discerning filter.

Try this:

In this chapter I mention 'Sue', who wanted to do something she didn't like because she wanted to earn some points with God. If you can think of a time you did something similar, write about that occasion. What was it? How did you feel after you did it?

When you hear the phrase "God loves you," what does that mean for you? Write about your feelings. Use the first person.

UNDERSTANDING LOVE

Love bears up under anything and everything that comes, is ever ready to believe the best of every person ...
— 1 Corinthians 13:7

How we see our earthly father can have a huge impact on how we see God. Acknowledging God as a loving father was difficult for me. I suppose those two words just did not go together—it seemed an oxymoron to say "loving father".

But love is not limited to a father-child relationship. Love is foundational in many relationships and if there is no love, then such relationships don't generally survive. When we grow up in an environment where love either does not exist, or, if it does, it is a toxic, destructive emotion that attempts to pass itself off as love, our entire understanding of love has to be reordered by God.

Many people want to do great things for God and they long for God to do a significant work in their lives. However, they try to avoid the love relationship. Christianity is not like any other religion. Christianity is about relationship, intimacy with the Creator of the universe—a love relationship that is initiated by Him. He created us for such a relationship, not for what we can do for Him. Until we get the love relationship right, nothing else will be right.

While Ross and I and our girls knew God called us to work in missions and to study at what is now Worldview Centre for Intercultural Studies but was then WEC Missionary Training College, we didn't have the love relationship sorted. God was to teach us about that in the days, months, and years to come. We hadn't thought much about missions before we moved to Ravenswood in Tasmania and started attending the Ravenswood Gospel Chapel. Many students from the local missionary training college attended the chapel, and we got to know them and sensed God stirring our hearts to be involved in missions. One student, Jenny, became a good friend while she was at college and stayed with us during one holiday break. It was when I was taking her home one day, as we turned into Station Road, St. Leonards, I distinctly heard what was like an audible voice say, "You'll be here one day."

God called us to go to South America, to Ecuador, to do medical work with HCJB. Lots of obstacles kept popping up, but less than a year after I heard that voice telling us we would be at WEC one day, we were there. Students and staff often say that college is like a huge pot of silver that is being refined; the heat is turned up and the hotter it gets, the more impurities come to the surface. It certainly was that for us, and we also learned that living in community can be a bit like the relationship between sandpaper and wood—the constant rubbing that occurs eventually smooths rough edges!

I had been a Christian for five years when we went to Ravenswood, and it was then that God began to reveal more of the spiritual battle we are in. It was a time, though, when some Christians were seeing demons behind every bush and were so busy casting out demons, they had no time for relationship with God. As Joyce Meyer says in one of her teachings, they were so busy casting out demons they didn't have time to clean up a sink full of dirty dishes! We got a bit caught up in this, and it's easy, in hindsight, to see how the enemy used this to distract me from what God really wanted—which was to draw me into a love relationship with Him. God's plan in revealing the nature of the battle was not to scare me but to show me that unless I was in Him and confident in my identity in Jesus, I would never defeat Satan. I didn't understand this. Fear still dominated all that I did.

Our time at Worldview continued to be a battle for me—a battle to understand God as Father. I just could not get my head around it. I would think, "Aha! I've got it," and just as quickly I would lose whatever thought I had, and I would be back in the same old place. I knew it was vitally important for me to understand this and frequently had conversations with God that went something like this:

"Well God, I know I should call you Father, but I'm not sure that's a good idea. Fathers aren't reliable as far as I can see. I'm not sure it's wise to think of You as Father—because it's making me more scared of you. I know you have a duty to look after me, but what happens if I do something You don't like? I'm not sure I can trust You. You say You'll be there with us in Ecuador, but what does that mean? You can be there and still not really be there. Grandpa was like that. How do I know You'll be any different? And what if I do something wrong, something that displeases You? Will You leave? Will You decide it's easier not to bother with me like dad did?"

Satan was having a heyday while I was going around and around the mountain with this sort of stuff. I had to know, really know, that God loved me before I could accept Him as Father in the true sense of that word; Satan would put thoughts in my mind such as, *How could God love me? He can't possibly love me.* And rather than refuse that thought, because I didn't know how to, I accepted it, allowed it not only to remain in my mind but to become a part of me, a belief about who I was, so I believed God didn't love me because I wasn't good enough. Something that has helped me understand this is learning about a part of our brain called the Reticular Activating System (RAS). Simply put, the RAS, among other things, is the automatic mechanism inside our brain that brings relevant information to our attention. It takes instructions from our conscious mind and passes them on to our subconscious, acting as a kind of filter. We can deliberately program our RAS by choosing the exact message we send from our conscious mind. When we do this the RAS then searches for relevant information to confirm this message. For instance, in my case, I programmed my RAS to search for information that would confirm the thought that God did not love me because I was not good enough. It is so important to understand this. The enemy does.

In the Garden of Eden Satan subtly planted doubt in Eve's mind, that lead to her questioning God's instructions. He does the same with us. I was already insecure. I didn't have past role models who modelled love, honesty, and truth. I was more than aware of my own failings and shortcomings, and I didn't have a relationship with the Father that gave me confidence to trust Him. What a mess! I had programmed my RAS to let what I perceived as vital through to alert my mind. However, with little understanding of taking captive every thought, and no real understanding of what it meant to have the mind of Christ (1 Corinthians 2:6)—that is, sharing the plan, purpose, and perspective of Christ, I was an easy target for whatever Satan wanted to plant in my mind.

While at college and in Costa Rica at language school, and then in Ecuador, I was trying very hard to be a good wife, a good mother, a good missionary, a good Christian—to be what was expected and what I thought I should be. I never asked God, "What do you really want of me?" And there was the problem. *I* was trying; *I* was doing all the work seeking approval, recognition, and acknowledgement that I did have something to offer that was valuable. I wanted God to approve of me, and the only way I knew to get His approval was to do things to please Him.

During all those years I studied the Bible, I read it in my quiet times, and I learned verses, but I don't remember having a hunger for it. I don't remember getting excited about it at all. Now I understand why. The Bible is only words on a page if there is no Holy Spirit revelation.

Understanding Love

Now, as I read, I am constantly amazed at the depth and wisdom, the relevance and utter brilliance of what I read. I often comment to Father that I'd really like a photographic memory. But the beautiful thing is we don't need such a memory because we have Holy Spirit. Jesus said the Holy Spirit would remind us of all that He (Jesus) said, that He would be our teacher and lead us into all truth.

I now have Holy Spirit revelation, but only because God, who loves me, did not give up on me. He persevered even when I turned my back on Him in the hard and challenging times after Ileana and Sarah died. Even when I turned from Him and refused to listen, He pursued me—when He says, "I will never leave you or forsake you," He means it. God is the Father I never had, and though I cannot see him as I would a flesh and blood father, He is no less real and present to me. After almost thirteen years in a wilderness of my own making, God, my Father, said to me, "That's enough, Karen. It's time to leave this behind, to move on. It's time to begin using all I have given you." God cared enough not to leave me in prison—so unlike my earthly father.

When Ross and I told Dad and my stepmother we were going to Ecuador as missionaries, they condemned us for taking the children, Miriam and Sarah, over there to such a dangerous place. And I suppose when our girls died, they felt justified in having made it clear to us they didn't approve. There was no love, no comfort from that quarter, when they were told about Illy and Sarah. Unlike Father God, who said, "I was *always* with you," my stepmother's response was one of anger, "How dare you ring and tell me this. I have enough on my plate looking after your father." We heard nothing more from either of them. I learned some time later that Dad had died. My niece, who lived in Melbourne, read of it in the newspaper and passed the news on to me.

Coming to know God as Father was a long and difficult road. I had no idea that my relationship or non-relationship with Dad could have such an impact on me throughout the rest of my life. Michael

Gurian, in his book *The Wonder of Girls: Understanding the Hidden Nature of Our Daughters,* beautifully describes the impact of a father on his daughter. He says,

> *A father who is honest with his daughter about his own flaws becomes her confidant. A father who remains stoic becomes her enigma to solve. A father who distances himself too greatly from his daughter becomes a burden she carries into life. If a father always finds time to cuddle, listen to, toss in the air, dance with, run alongside, coach, comfort, and protect his daughter, he will give her the gift of life he is built to give. If a father withholds nothing, teaching his daughter the life skills she needs to know, he shares an active kind of respect for variety in a girl's developing self. If a father competes with his daughter in games, but especially when she is young lets her win her share of races, he is showing both his own humility and her potential. And as a father helps a daughter enter the world of sexuality, romance, and then marriage, a man becomes more than an arm to walk down the aisle with—he becomes, in his daughter's mind, fearless ...*

Linda Shierse Leonard, a well-known psychologist, begins her book, *The Wounded Woman* with this description of hurting women:

> *Every week women come into my office suffering from a poor self-image, from the inability to form lasting relationships, or from a lack of confidence in their ability to work and function in the world. On the surface these women often appear quite successful—confident businesswomen, contented housewives, carefree students, swinging divorcees. But underneath the veneer of success or contentment is the injured self, the hidden despair, the feelings of loneliness and isolation, the fear of abandonment and rejection, the tears of rage.*

Understanding Love

She goes on to explain what her book is about: this hidden despair, the deep woundedness of these women, often stems from a damaged relationship with their fathers. Leonard suggests that when a father is damaged in his own psychological development, he is not able to give his daughter the love and guidance she needs.

It's easy for us to dismiss this as just another secular theory that doesn't have any significance for Christians. After all, we think we have God's forgiveness towards us, and this makes it possible for us to forgive our fathers for any failings. We need to be careful in dismissing this theory so blithely. H. Norman Wright, a well-known and trusted Christian counsellor, says in *Healing for the Father Wound* that our fathers shape who we are whether they are absent or play a central part in our life. The lack of fathering plagues all women, including Christian women.

Healing Place is the name of the business God called me into. Healing Place has been a vehicle through which I have helped deeply wounded men and women to a place of hope and healing spiritually, emotionally, and sometimes even physically. The deep healing that needs to happen begins in the heart. Many of us have friends or relatives who have experienced physical heart problems, or we may have experienced one ourselves. In order for us to get on with life, we need to have the problem fixed because we just can't function well if our heart is not working as it should. Recently, a Christian friend and pastor was sharing how God is changing her spiritual heart. She said she realised there was so much work to do to make her heart whole that she asked God to take the old heart completely out and replace it with a new one—a heart transplant!

I was diagnosed with a physical heart problem just before the pandemic hit our world. Until then I had knowledge about heart health gained from my years as a nurse, however since the diagnosis I often reflect on how important the health of our heart is to our overall well-being. It is also easier for me to see that just as the physical heart can suffer numerous ailments that need to be corrected, so our emotional lives can suffer various maladies of the heart that arise because of faulty relationships. When I sat down to read what I have written here, I was reminded of a chat with my cardiologist. We were talking about grief and my recent book, A Grief Revealed. He asked if I had heard of Takotsubo Cardiomyopathy. I hadn't. He then asked if I'd heard of Broken Heart Syndrome. Of course, I had. It happens they are one and the same thing. Broken Heart Syndrome is temporary, and not usually fatal, but it does need targeted treatment. The usual cause of this syndrome is a stressful situation and extreme emotions. Eventually, the heart heals but until it does the sufferer cannot move on with life. And just as you can't move on with life with a faulty physical heart, no matter what the cause, you can't move on with a damaged emotional heart. H. Norman Wright writes of some common heart problems in daughters. A daughter with a bruised heart feels beaten down and never feels good enough to live up to the expectations of those around her, especially her father. She feels ashamed, fearful, and insecure, and she is afraid to try in case she makes a mistake or isn't successful. The one with a bruised heart is in survival mode, believing she must fend for herself because no one else cares enough, and she often withdraws into herself as a way of not being hurt. She is usually sensitive, despairing, and lives without hope. The daughter with a performance heart drives herself to succeed because she is afraid of failure or disappointment and wants to prove to her father she can—he didn't provide what she needs, so she will get it herself. This daughter lives with feelings of inadequacy, of not being able to measure up in the eyes of her dad. The daughter with a hardened heart has been terribly hurt, so much so that she shuts down emotionally and cuts herself off from her heart. The one emotion she allows herself to feel is anger, and this comes out very strongly. The addicted heart, says Wright, is another hurt heart, one that latches on to people, things, activities, food, anything that will cover the hurt inside. Everything is done to excess to cover the disappointments this daughter has experienced. Perhaps you know someone who has a heart like one of those described above, or perhaps it is you with the heart problem. God is bigger than all the disappointments and pain we experience; when we know Him as Father, He takes care of us, loves us, and affirms us—and heals our hurts.

My heart struggled with elements of all the things described above and without realising it, I was allowing the things of the past to have a strong, limiting influence in my life. I was living for now, wanting to do things for God to make things right. But God has created us for eternity, He has put eternity in our hearts and this time on earth is when He develops our character into His likeness. It wasn't until September 2007, 29 years after becoming a Christian, that I truly understood the truth of Ephesians 1:4-5: "Even as [in His love] He chose us [actually picked us out for Himself as His own] in Christ before the foundation of the world, that we should be holy (consecrated and set apart for Him) and blameless in His sight, even above reproach, before Him in love. For He foreordained us (destined us, planned in love for us) to be adopted (revealed) as His own children through Jesus Christ, in accordance with the purpose of His will [because it pleased Him and was His kind intent]."

God has loved me from before time, since even before the foundation of the world. He actually chose me for Himself in Christ Jesus and planned for me to be adopted as His daughter—because it pleased Him. These words have become highly significant to me since that time. Other words that became significant are these: "Today is the beginning of a new walk for you. There is no turning back."

The above statement came from God through a lady a couple of seats along from me, as I worshipped at Edge Church in Adelaide on May 20th, 2007. I went to the church primarily to check it out and make sure it was OK for Miriam, our daughter, who had been glowing in her praise of Edge. I went not to worship and hear from God, but to vet the place. God, as gracious as He is, reached out to me and touched me in a powerful way—through the people, the message, and the music. Warmth flowed through me like never before, tears welled up, and so did an intense desire to know God and His plans for me.

Something was happening deep within my spirit as God touched me. People who had never met me before prayed for me, and a woman who saw me for the first time that morning turned to me and said, "God wants you to stay close to Him. To rest and relax in Him." Such words went directly to my burdened heart, and the depth of the touching was such that the emotion overflowed in tears—tears of joy and thanksgiving for the faithfulness of God and for His patience with me. It was then that I heard God say enough was enough, that it was time for me to stop what I was doing and move on to what He had for me. In my spirit I turned and faced Jesus, who was standing with arms outstretched, looking at me with such love in His eyes that I felt the fire of that love reach into every part of me. He stood and waited, waited for me to move towards Him. His voice washed over me: "I have always been with you; I never left you." I walked towards Him, in to waiting arms that circled me, drawing me to rest in Him, welcoming me home. No turning back.

Grace allows people to belong before they believe (1 Timothy 1:12-14), and I began to think that perhaps I had not believed but only pretended to do so. In 1 Corinthians 15:8, Paul calls himself *"abnormally born"* and goes on to write, "and last of all he appeared to me also, as to one prematurely and born dead." Literally, Paul is referring to a dead foetus—one born with no spirit—far from the grace of God. But he continues, saying that "by the grace of God (the unmerited favour and blessing) I am what I am, and His grace toward me was not [found to be] for nothing (fruitless and without effect)." That day at Edge I knew the belonging; this was my Father who had never abandoned me. I was home, and I believed.

In his book *The God-shaped Brain*, Timothy Jennings proposes that changing one's view of God can transform one's life. When God spoke to me telling me, "That's enough," it was a significant moment for me that caused a loud "Aha!" to happen. It was a moment when the left and right hemispheres of my brain became integrated so that my view of God changed. The Truth obliterated the lie that I had

Understanding Love

believed about Him. Prior to this moment, I had been living with the image of God as He was to me when I was growing up—a fearsome, frowning God who was annoyed and frustrated with my failings and poor choices, a God shaking His finger at me and berating me for never quite making it, watching and waiting for the next mistake, the next stuff up. But this God who clapped His hands and firmly stated, "That's enough, Karen," was not frowning, not fierce. He didn't yell at me that He'd had enough of me and was washing His hands of me if I didn't stop the nonsense. Rather, He took me by the hand and said, "Come with Me. Let me show you what I have for you. It's a good life, where peace and joy prevail. Let Me teach you all the good things I've had planned for you from the beginning of time." This was a loving Father wanting only the best for His daughter.

At an Edge Church conference later that year I had a supernatural experience that again seemed to me a gift from God. A demonstration of His grace towards me and another confirmation that He loves me. At the beginning of an evening session, we were worshipping and praising God in song. I stood with many others with hands raised, rejoicing in being there together in worship. Suddenly I was at the back of a room that could only have been God's throne room. It was immense and seemed to have no boundaries. People filled this room, and the sound was like nothing I had ever heard. Far in front of me I saw three thrones with angels coming and going and people moving back and forth; then as I looked at the sea of people a little closer to me, a young woman with long, straight, dark hair turned toward me. It was Sarah. Her face shone and her smile was brighter than the brightest lamp I have seen. My field of vision narrowed, and it was just Sarah and me.

"This is what we do here, Mum. Come and join us."

I thought for a moment that I would have a heart attack or something else drastic would happen and that it was my time to go home to heaven. Then I was back in the auditorium at Edge Church, and the conference session was beginning.

Try this:

Write about something that was significant to you in this chapter.

Consider the hearts described in this chapter. What is your heart like? Describe it. How does it link with your relationship with your father? With God? Be specific and honest with yourself. Write in the first person.

FREEDOM

And you shall know the Truth, and the Truth will set you free.
— John 8:32

William Wallace was a hero to the Scottish people. He refused to bow down to the English, whose one desire was to destroy the Scots as a people and to cause them to submit totally to English rule. For years, they were turned from their homes on a whim of an English lord, beaten, ridiculed, and forced to forsake their cultural identity. Wallace wanted freedom for his people and was willing to put his life on the line for it. A scene in the movie, Braveheart, that remains etched in my memory is of Wallace and the outnumbered, motley crowd that was the Scottish army standing proudly before the well-trained and well-equipped English. Bold and focused, Wallace's battle cry is *'Freedom!'* His men take up the cry and it reverberates across the battleground; a deep, visceral thundering of intent that shakes the enemy even as they uneasily stand their ground in the face of such passion.

As the Victorious Ministry Through Christ team prophesied over me at the first prayer school I attended in September 2007, the cry that came from deep within me was just such a cry. I felt it rumbling up from within, and nothing I could have done would have stopped it from coming out. *"Freedom!"* It was a proclamation that shook the room, pushed me to my feet and caused my arms to lift in thanksgiving to God for what He had done. For the first time in my life, I was thrown to the floor by the Holy Spirit and while I was there, He spoke to me, calling me to join Him in setting prisoners free, healing the broken hearted, unstopping deaf ears and opening blind eyes. As He spoke, I had a sense of something strong as steel being poured into my body. From the feet up there was a strengthening, like the reinforcing that goes into buildings. One of the team who had prayed for me whispered, *"There's no turning back"*. A little later he returned and repeated the command, *"There's no turning back."* I heard those words for the first time at Edge Church earlier that year; God reinforced this command, this new way of living, twice more and I knew then that perfect love, the love of a Father, had cast out fear, and trust was pouring into the places left empty. For the first time in my life, I think, I knew what it was to be at peace.

God first spoke to me in 2004 about using what had happened in my life to help others, but it took three years, almost to the day, for Him to bring me to the place where I was ready to join Him. Then in 2006, God spoke through Tim, one of the pastors at Gateway Baptist Church, about the plans God had for my life. It was something else I put on the shelf, as I wasn't ready for it.

It's hard to believe I ignored God for so long. And it's only His grace that has me here now, free from all that sin had me locked into. The scariest thing is that I was a Christian. I was a missionary. I prayed, I read the Bible, I even studied the Word. Ross and I had Bible Studies in our home. I was part of the worship team at English Fellowship Church, but I was still captive to the rejection, the pain, the fear, and the anger that had become a part of me before I knew Jesus. I remember the futility I felt as I tried to change myself. I was open to the lies and deception of Satan, who had me believing that this was the way life was, and I just had to make the best of it.

Freedom

That moment in which revelation came, when I *knew* without any doubt that I was free, was an amazing time. Imagine being a prisoner of war, or of a terrorist group, locked away in a dark and hidden place, hoping but not knowing whether negotiations are taking place, uncertainty gnawing away at you day after day as you wonder if anyone cares enough to want you free. Then one day, after what seems a lifetime of waiting, while you sit there in your cell anticipating another day like all the others, too afraid to hope, to believe that you will ever again live outside the crushing walls of your prison, you hear the thud of booted feet coming towards your cell. They stop outside your door, a key clanks and grates in the lock, the door swings open and a voice growls, *"Get up, you are free to go."* Everything in you wants to believe this is real, not another trick, but doubt and unbelief are very strong, so you sit, unable to move. *"Get up and get out or I will lock this door again and you will never leave!"*

Heart pounding, breathing rapidly so that you are almost dizzy, you leap up and move fast towards the door still expecting this to be a trick and the guard to slam the door in your face. But he doesn't; instead, he shoves you roughly towards the entrance, only a short distance away. Still, doubt is strong, it's been too long, and freedom seems no more than an impossible dream. The closer you get to the entrance, the more aware you are of a strange sound, the slow slap, slap of heavy blades turning—a helicopter? Your heart beats even faster. Maybe, maybe … You step outside into a blinding sun-filled desert and there, only metres away, is a flight to freedom and standing, waiting with the door open, is your commanding officer.

Freedom! Now you believe it. Someone cared enough to do what was necessary to set you free. Freedom, no longer a dream, is now a reality. All you have to do is leave the place that has held you prisoner and step through the other door that has opened to you. How would you feel? Would you take those few extra steps and leap through the door that is waiting for you?

What reality are you living in? The revelation that came for me was that I had lived for a very long time in a reality that was not truth; my reality was a lie, a deception. Nevertheless, it *was* a reality.

Freedom comes from knowing God and knowing that Jesus has done it all—done all that is necessary to break you out of prison, to cut the chains off your wrists and ankles so you can walk free in confidence and strength. I stayed in deception, not realising the cell door wasn't locked and the chains could easily be thrown off, that all I had to do was trust God and step out of them, just as Peter did when he stepped out of the boat and onto the water in response to Jesus calling him. A great verse that Holy Spirit showed me is Psalm 40:6, which says, *"Sacrifice and offering You do not desire, nor have You delight in them; You have given me the capacity to hear and obey [Your law, a more valuable service than] burnt offerings and sin offerings [which] You do not require."*

Those words clearly tell us that when God calls us to do something, He not only gives us the capacity to hear but to obey as well; He gives us all we need to do what He is calling us to do. The day freedom became my reality was just the beginning. To stay free, a soldier needs to know his enemy, their strategies and tactics, and then deliberately choose to avoid walking into the traps the enemy has set. A news item caught my eye recently. Apparently, in my home state, almost 50 percent of prisoners freed from jail reoffend and are back within two years. A Salvation Army officer said it was because it was easier to be in prison where there is certainty and stability than it is to be out in the world. Prisoners long to be out of prison and free, but they don't know what to do to remain free; prison doesn't prepare them to live as free people and so they don't plan and think about how to avoid those things that put them in prison in the first place. Eventually they reoffend and end up back in prison.

Faith is the method God has designed for us to receive all He has for us; all He wants to give us. Faith is God's gift to us to help us stay out of prison. It makes sense, then, that acquiring faith, a gift from

God, and developing it is important to the Father. And given that doubt leads to unbelief, it makes sense that this would be a tactic of the enemy to keep us from all that God wants for us.

Earlier I said that on that day when freedom became a reality for me, I knew *without doubt* I was free. In that moment I reached out and accepted the gift of faith from the Father that had been planted in me right back when I first accepted Christ as my Saviour. It was as I did that, as I stepped into the reality of truth, that Holy Spirit began reinforcing the new me, the warrior me. I moved from the role of oppressed prisoner to strong and victorious warrior. The sense of steel being poured into me was a manifestation of what was happening in my spirit.

I had never spoken in tongues before this. Very early in our married life, Ross and I met a young couple who insisted we needed to speak in tongues to demonstrate we were saved. They attempted to get me to speak a new language through many and various means—none of them successful. Their insistence that I must not be saved caused me to turn from ever consciously considering tongues again. Yet during this time of transformation, which is what it was for me, as radical as a caterpillar turning into a butterfly, I found myself praying in a strange language. It was an almost harsh, forceful sound that caused me to feel a sense of authority as I spoke out and to want to stand tall. When I asked Father if I could have a softer, gentler language, He responded, *"I have given you a warrior tongue."* And that's just what I needed at the time.

A few years ago, while participating in a workshop, God gave me a gift—a gift of remembering. I don't often think of my childhood and when I do I tend to remember people rather than happenings. God took the pain from the memories, pain that was connected to the sense of rejection, abandonment, indifference, and unworthiness. Now I can think of Mum and Dad and others and love them with His love. That day, as part of a group exercise I looked at those who were important to me in the first few years of my life. I was drawing my mind map of people and events that were significant in the first five years when into my mind popped some of my friends from when I lived in Williamsford, a now non-existent mining town on the rugged west coast of Tasmania. As I thought about them, I remembered special days—hot summer days, brilliant blue, cloudless-sky days when we would go to a water hole, which had formed in the local river where we could safely play and swim.

My wet feet slip in the plastic sandals I always wore to protect my feet from the rocky bottom. Water glistens and sparkles in the brilliant sunshine. We splash and scoop the water and it flashes like diamonds as it flies through the air so that the surrounding trees take on the sparkle too as they shimmer and shift in the slight breeze. Laughter reverberates around the sheltered place, and I am happy. I am free and joyful, being me, Karen, a child being a child—not the rejected daughter of Doug, or the abandoned child of Ann. Just me as God made me to be—free. A deep sense of peace pervades me, and I am grateful for the freedom that is mine again.

I lost that freedom when I was about four and a half. I lost it to fear, and it became imprisoned in a dark place that didn't see the sunlight and blue skies, a place where I couldn't wave my hands with joyful abandon because they hung down in defeat and uncertainty, shackled by the iron of others' harsh words. But God rescued me and brought me out of that dark place—freedom is mine again and I am me, who God made me to be. I can wave my hands and lift them in praise, and I can laugh happily because I am free. No matter what is happening, and when life is not simple or easy, I can lift my hands and laugh with joy because I am free! I remember those days and I smile. Thank you, God, for the gift of remembering. The revelation that we are free is just the beginning. Staying free requires commitment, and it requires that we recognise that we are warriors, that we know who we are in Christ, and live in that place of authority and victory. "Now the Lord is the Spirit, and where the Spirit of the Lord is, there is liberty *(emancipation from bondage, freedom)*" (2 Corinthians 3:17).

Freedom

Holy Spirit leads us into all truth. Life in the Spirit enables us to live in freedom. He is in me, transforming and renewing, doing what needs to be done to expose the new creation I have become in Christ. Living in freedom is an ongoing exercise, a spiritual discipline. Spiritual discipline can only flow out of relationship with God though, otherwise it becomes works, a duty, following rules and regulations in the hope that you might gain the prize. I tried the disciplines. When we were at WEC Missionary Training College, one of the texts we were required to read was Richard Foster's *Celebration of Discipline: The Path to Spiritual Growth*. I read it then and tried to put some of the disciplines into practice. After a few weeks it was too difficult so, together with the book that was read and ticked off on the reading list, the disciplines themselves were ticked off as done. In 2012, when I offered to teach about Spiritual Disciplines to the first-year students at Worldview, I was conscious as I prepared that I was now living out a number of those spiritual disciplines. As I grew in knowledge and understanding of walking in the Spirit (Galatians 5:16), as I learned from Holy Spirit, I had incorporated His teachings into my life without realising it, and they had become a natural part of my spiritual walk. Freedom is about life in the Spirit. Without Holy Spirit we cannot walk in freedom. Jesus explained this in John 7:37-39:

> *Now on the final and most important day of the Feast, Jesus stood, and He cried in a loud voice, If any man is thirsty, let him come to Me and drink! He who believes in Me [who cleaves to and trusts in and relies on Me] as the Scripture has said, From his innermost being shall flow [continuously] springs and rivers of living water. But He was speaking here of the Spirit, Whom those who believed (trusted, had faith) in Him were afterward to receive. For the [Holy] Spirit had not yet been given, because Jesus was not yet glorified (raised to honour).*

He also spoke of this in John 4:14: "But whoever takes a drink of the water that I will give him shall never, no never, be thirsty any more. But the water that I will give him shall become a spring of water welling up (flowing, bubbling) [continually] within him unto (into, for) eternal life." If we are to be filled with living water, which is the Spirit, there must be room in us for this water. And anything that might stop its flow has to be cleaned out so that the living water can flow freely. When I believed in and on Jesus and came to faith in Him, Father wanted to fill me with living water, but first he had to clean out everything that was taking up room. He wanted to dig into me and remove the dirt, get rid of the fear, and replace it with love, remove the anxiety and replace it with trust, throw out the doubt and fill me with faith. And He wanted me to have the oil of joy instead of being miserable and a spirit of praise instead of a spirit of depression.

To walk in freedom means partnering with God and allowing Him to do what He needs to do. While all those negative and destructive things are in residence, we cannot live the abundant life that is ours in Jesus, the life of freedom and wholeness, of *"righteousness, peace and joy in the Holy Spirit"*—kingdom life. I had to learn that God loves me and wants the best for me, and learn to trust Him before I could allow Him to do what He needed to do. I needed to see Him as a loving Father. And, despite being a Christian since 1978, it wasn't until 2007 that I came into that relationship with Him.

Through Holy Spirit, I now walk in freedom. All those things that have been displaced, thrown out, and evicted know they no longer have authority over me. While I allowed them to remain, they knew that gave them rights over certain parts of my life and a significant outworking of this was the opposition to all that God wanted to do in me. Some, particularly fear and intimidation, attempt to return, not as often as they used to; but Holy Spirit gives discernment, and He reminds me of my authority. I don't have to bow down to these negative and destructive influences, but it is my choice. And I choose

Freedom

life in the Spirit, not the living death I once allowed. I deliberately, each time a choice is required, choose freedom.

Try this:

Write about anything that is significant for you in this chapter. Why is it significant?

If you are, right now, in a dark place, is there anything in this chapter that helped you see that you don't need to remain there? If so, what was it? How did it help you? Write about what is happening for you right now.

ECUADOR – INTRODUCTION TO MISSIONARY LIFE

Be gentle and forbearing with one another, and if one has a difference against another, readily pardoning each other; even as the Lord has forgiven you, so must you also forgive.

— Colossians 3:13

Flying into Quito for the first time was an unreal and scary experience. I couldn't look because it seemed impossible not to wipe out numerous buildings as we came in to land. The airport was right in the middle of the city, built on a high plateau, and as the plane dropped in altitude and the wheels came down, you held your breath wondering if this time your plane might be one that overshot the runway to plough into the neighbouring houses! It was also the first time I had experienced a planeload of people erupting in exuberant clapping, but they did, and almost every time we landed in Quito the response was the same! We were excited to arrive, finally, in Ecuador. Our rose-coloured glasses were firmly in place, and we sailed happily through customs despite being very tired. This, after all, was where we would do great things for God.

We remained in Quito for a couple of days to do all the official things. Our excitement to see Shell, where we were to spend our first term, was dampened a little for me when I realised what the road was like that we had to traverse to get there. I do not like heights, and I prefer to keep my eyes closed if we travel close to the edge of a road that drops off sharply. After leaving the town of Baños, my eyes were closed for almost all the rest of the trip.

We spent our first few weeks in the home of a family who were on furlough, Home Ministry Assignment. What was to be our home was one of two apartments on the bottom floor of the old Ev Fuller building. It was one of the original houses that had been home to the martyred missionaries who gave their lives to take the Gospel to the Waorani people. Nate Saint was one of those missionaries, who had, to some extent, been raised to idol status, something I'm sure they would not have wanted. Elisabeth Elliott tells their story in *Through Gates of Splendour*.

The apartment was old, termite-ridden, and smelly. I remember walking into the bathroom for the first time and being almost overwhelmed by what smelled like stale urine. Ugh!! I was immediately transported back to early days as a nursing student when I worked in what was then called the geriatric ward. The apartment needed a lot of work to be made habitable, and we discovered that it was up to Ross to organise it and do most of the work. Two Ecuadorian guys helped when they could be spared from the hospital. Grace certainly was not at work in me back then, or if it was, it was in a limited way. I was easily offended and quick to make it known, sad to say. I was annoyed that nothing had been done before we arrived. In fact, I couldn't understand how they expected Ross to work at the hospital and also get our apartment ready. We had no furniture either, so we had to depend on others who were leaving to sell us theirs or travel to Quito for things. We didn't have a vehicle, and it was not easy to take

Ecuador – Introduction to missionary life

the time to go to the capital. I decided I would write to our supporters and let them know what we needed, including a washing machine. Imagine my annoyance and how I bristled when I received a letter from someone who wasn't a financial supporter but had decided to write to us, suggesting I should, like all good missionaries, take the clothes to the river to wash! My immediate response was to write back and make very clear to the gentleman that the river was so contaminated I could not wash clothes in it—even if I could navigate the steep banks to get to it in the first place.

We were very dependent on others and my perception was that not everyone was helpful. Rosie and Dave took us under their wings and were great. If it hadn't been for them, we may well have left early. One couple jokingly declared, *"We had to fend for ourselves too, you know! It's the initiation."* I wasn't impressed, and I didn't laugh. The rose-coloured glasses were off, and I wasn't too happy with what I saw without them. I mentioned earlier that I decided to write to our supporters telling them what we needed, but I didn't stop to talk to God about it at all. I had an attitude that I still see in some people in fulltime work, and that is that since we are serving God, people have an obligation to support and help us. This attitude was often cleverly cloaked in what I consider pseudo-spirituality. I would say I was trusting God, but in reality, I was depending on and trusting people and my own ability to make things happen. Yes, God called us, and He said He would provide, but very quickly I took over and tried to do it for Him—just in case He fell down on the job. I can see now that because I was let down so many times in my life, I was just waiting and expecting that God would do the same, and I didn't want to give Him that chance if I could help it. So when we arrived in Shell and had to make our own home from scratch, instead of talking to God and asking Him to provide as He had said He would, I ranted and railed and took offence that we were treated so poorly (my perception) and subconsciously added this to the list of reasons why I couldn't trust anyone, even God. When I stopped long enough to look outside of myself, I understood that everyone was busy and we eventually settled into life in Shell, becoming a part of the community as best we could.

We had been in Shell a few months when we learned that Mum was in hospital in Hobart. Before we left for Ecuador, she and I had begun to be more open with each other. Mum hated when I mentioned Jesus and wasn't happy that I no longer considered myself a Catholic, but she had come to see that Ross was a good man who cared for me, and that perhaps the fact that he didn't smoke, drink, and swear was a good thing! Before we married, Mum was often derogatory about Ross. I think for her, the ultimate insult was to say he was like my father, although he isn't at all. She appreciated that he would do things for her when we visited and acknowledged that our marriage might just be OK. I looked forward to spending time with her when we returned from Ecuador and perhaps even helping her see her need for Jesus.

It was a shock to hear that she had collapsed, and the diagnosis was a ruptured cerebral aneurysm with resultant subarachnoid haemorrhage (bleeding into the brain). I knew from my nursing experience that she was lucky to be alive. News came slowly as there was no Internet in Shell and phones were unreliable; mostly the news came via people travelling from Quito. This meant it was always a little behind. I was a couple of months pregnant with Ileana and had not even written to Mum to let her know, thinking there would always be time once I was sure everything was OK.

A week after we first heard, the news came that mum had died. The day was drizzly and grey, the surrounding mountains barely visible through the mists that shrouded them; it was as miserable as I felt. I walked around Shell trying to understand why God allowed it to happen. Why, when we were just starting to get to know each other in a meaningful way, had God taken Mum? Confusion turned to anger—my way of coping with things I didn't understand. I was angry with God for allowing this to happen. I had prayed and trusted Him to make things right between Mum and me, and now there was

Ecuador - Introduction to missionary life

no hope. I was also angry with my parents-in-law, wrongfully blaming them for being too slow to pass on the information about the gravity of Mum's condition, which meant I couldn't get to a telephone to call the hospital and at least let Mum know I did love her even if I couldn't be there.

My sister, who sat by Mum's bedside, was angry and resentful that when mum did speak, she asked for me, which made me feel terribly guilty that I wasn't even able to let her hear my voice. The relationship between my sister and me had never been strong since we really didn't know each other that well, and this didn't help at all. Trust took another blow as I tried to make sense of this through my own ways of understanding it, and just couldn't.

Kim and I missed a lot of years because of resentment and other toxic, negative feelings birthed in our childhood. Through no fault of our own, we were separated when very young. The gap that grew was too wide to be bridged without help, help we did not receive once we were brought together again, so while we lived in the same house for several years, there was no connection.

Knowing God and trusting Him would have made a huge difference when Mum was dying. I was so caught up in myself and unused to God's grace and love working in me, let alone through me, so I missed seeing this time as an opportunity for Kim and me to come together and instead focused only on the unfairness of what was happening while I was so far away. I didn't even consider contacting Kim to let her know I appreciated all she had done for Mum and that she was there when Mum needed her; instead, I lived in resentment that I couldn't be there.

God demonstrated His grace when, in 2009, several years after we returned from Ecuador, I felt a strong urge to contact Kim as I planned a trip to Hobart for a weekend course. I was hesitant as we had been back in Australia for thirteen years and hadn't seen each other even once. By this time, I was learning to respond to what I believed was Holy Spirit prompting me, speaking to me, so I called

Kim. She was excited; I could hear it in her voice as she immediately suggested I stay with her.

The weekend was great even though I was at courses throughout the day. Still, we had time to talk, really talk, and connected in a way we never had before. Kim was excited, and we made plans for me to stay with her again in a couple of months' time. Two weeks later, on a Tuesday evening at 11 p.m. I received a phone call from a neighbour of Kim's: *"You need to come down, Kim's been rushed to the Royal."* I had no idea what I would find but arrived at the Royal Hobart Hospital in time to attend a meeting with the medical team, a meeting in which I met my niece for the first time and realised that the meeting was about how soon to turn off the life support. Kim had suffered a massive cerebral bleed from a ruptured aneurysm just as Mum had, but Kim never had a chance of waking up from it. The sense of God's presence throughout this difficult time, and the reality of His grace at work to allow Kim and me that time before she died, were a stark contrast to how I was when Mum died. I sat with Kim for a while before they turned off the life support. There was time to cry, and to ask her forgiveness for many things. From a clinical perspective, she wouldn't have heard me, but I know God is greater than the clinical perspective, and I believe Kim did know I was there and heard my heart speaking to her.

After Mum died, I came to accept that she was gone, but never really addressed the feelings I had towards God. I've learned that when I struggle with something I tend to throw myself into work or ministry. It's a way of running from something rather than facing it. It doesn't work though, because eventually whatever it is catches up, and it's usually when you are in a corner with no way of running further. The problem is that wherever you go, there *you* are! Joyce Meyer, in one of her teachings, talks of the giants in your life, those things that you just do not want to face because they are too big, or too hard to deal with, and I have come to see that there were lots of giants in my life. Thank goodness God didn't give up on me and He showed me

Ecuador – Introduction to missionary life

I am a giant killer! It just took thirteen years for me to allow Him to speak to me again and for me to begin to learn the lessons that gave me the confidence to start facing those giants. I wonder how different our time in Ecuador might have been if I had been a giant killer back then instead of someone constantly overwhelmed by the sheer hugeness of the giants.

It's amazing that when God calls us, He never abandons us. Even when I was struggling with so much 'stuff' I had a reasonably effective ministry. God continued to work through me even though I wasn't whole. And He, in His grace, does that. If He waited for us to be perfect, I doubt there'd be much happening. I had Bible studies with some of the ladies from the military base, I taught infection-control principles to hospital staff, and I even acted as interpreter and translator for some of the doctors from the US or Canada who were in Shell on short-term contracts and didn't speak Spanish. One of the things I really enjoyed doing was writing for *Amigos Magazine*, HCJB's magazine for the health care division in Ecuador. I told stories of the way God was active in the life of many people, rescuing them from the darkness of being controlled by shamans or witch doctors, healing them physically through the care they received at the Hospital Vozandes–Shell, and often drawing them into new life in Jesus. I realise now, that even as I wrote those stories, I was a little removed from them, from the reality of the miraculous that was so much a part of what God was doing. Even as I recounted stories of the miraculous in peoples' lives, even knowing the power of God and despite the power confrontations I had when we were at WEC and even before then, and despite the promise that He would be with us, I was still hesitant to trust God to take care of us.

In my primary school days at St. Brigid's Convent, New Norfolk, as we walked to Mass every Friday, we played a game called The Devil Will Get You. It was a silly game where we had to make sure we didn't step on the cracks in the concrete footpath, because if you did, the devil would get you. So we bounced and jumped, seriously intent on getting to the church for Mass before the devil could get us. We did this with a fierce determination that belied that it was only a game; for some of us, the seriousness underlying our efforts was, I think, a symptom of something deeper.

After believing on and in Jesus and right up until I was totally set free in 2007, I was like that little girl, doing my very best to avoid everything that would mean the devil would get me. I had an intense fear of Satan that, at times, almost paralysed me. Despite this, God gave me an ability to write about spiritual things in a way that came out of an understanding of how the devil works, and how intense that battle is.

While at WEC, I had some dramatic confrontations with Satan. Despite not wanting anything to do with that side of things, God allowed me to experience the heat of the battle, which, I guess had started when we were still living at Ravenswood. Not wanting anything to do with something doesn't make it go away, and so I continued to learn what power there is in the name of Jesus—as Ross and I discovered when we were attacked fiercely after my grandma died. I dreamed one night that I was in a very deep and dark pit. The sides were steep and there was no way to get out; above, there was only darkness. I was overwhelmed by fear, and as I cringed from a malevolent presence, a great whirlwind came, hurling dirt, dead leaves, and other debris at me even as I felt the force of it pulling at my hair and my clothes, sucking me into its centre. I tried to cry out, but it was as though something had its hands around my throat so that I could barely breathe, let alone call out. Yet, with as much force as I had left, I managed to croak in a broken, scarcely audible rasp "Jesus!" It wasn't even a shout, just a desperate cry, yet immediately the wind stopped. A supernatural stillness fell, and when I dropped my hands from my eyes, I looked up and saw a hand reaching down into the pit, and above where there had been only darkness, there was now the face of Jesus.

The dream was significant for several reasons. I saw myself in a place of no escape; the malevolence of that presence was almost palpable.

Ecuador – Introduction to missionary life

I knew whatever it was hated me with such a passion that only my total destruction would appease it, and I felt powerless to do anything. The fear was so overwhelming that all I wanted to do was hide from it, yet its power was such that I was paralysed, unable to move. As all-encompassing and oppressive as this evil was, the name of Jesus was enough to send it running. Despite everything that was thrown at me and despite my own weakness, my faith in Jesus came through and He responded to that faith. His strength was made perfect in my weakness. Something else significant here is that Jesus dealt with the evil that had tried to destroy me, but He didn't just snatch me out of the pit—I had to decide to take His hand. I have found over and over that when we call out to God, He does help us, but He only goes so far. He expects us to do our bit too.

Joyce Meyer has a teaching called "'New Level, New Devil." I don't think that's quite right—the devil is always the same devil, but the battle we are in goes to a new level along with our promotion. Even now I am sometimes surprised at the viciousness of the attack and can be knocked off my feet so to speak, for a while, until I realise what is happening. When we were in Ecuador though, I played right into the enemy's hands because I really was ignorant of the strategies and tactics he uses. I wasn't aware that fear is one of his most used soldiers and one that is usually the first to attack. Often, fear is such a strong adversary and so successful that there is no need to send in reinforcements.

Who would believe that God could actually do something through me with all the doubt, fear, lack of trust, and uncertainty that seemed to plague me? But He did. I became very close to one Shell family. Mery and Gonzales have become very dear to me, and I met them because I wanted to write a story about their daughter Jessica.

It wasn't until many years later that I learned Mery gave her life to Jesus because of the relationship we had. Once again, God's grace was at work in that even when I really didn't have a true knowledge and understanding of Him as a loving Father, He honoured the attempts

I made in my ignorance. Mery was pregnant with their fourth child when we met and they named her Carina after me, and I learned later, when I returned to Ecuador in 2012, that they named their next daughter Miriam, after our Miriam. Mery now works at a Compassion International Project near Shell. Our relationship remains special.

Our time in Shell taught us a lot, but we still had so much to learn. We made great friends, we struggled, and we laughed and cried together with our fellow missionaries who were from several countries: New Zealand, Canada, Finland, Holland, Germany, the USA, England, and Australia. We had a great team and there was a real sense of working together, with no one member of the team more important than the others. If anyone needed help, the call would go out, and there was always a response, a willingness to help each other. At times, blood was needed for a transfusion, and those of us with the correct blood type would head over to the hospital where the blood would barely leave the body before being given to the one who needed it. Despite this, we were still seeing things through our eyes, not God's, and although the rose-coloured glasses were off, we still weren't seeing a true picture of what was happening, so we remained very set on doing things our way, not really understanding what it meant to be led by the Spirit.

Try this:

Have you ever been so overwhelmed by fear that you can barely make a sound? When was it, and what was happening? Did God intervene for you? If so, how did He intervene? What was it like for you? Write about the experience you had.

Numerous times in His Word, God tells us not to be afraid because He is always with us—and He will not allow us to be tempted beyond what we can stand. Write about what that means for you. Write from the heart, not what you believe is expected of you—be honest.

HOME MINISTRY ASSIGNMENT AND BACK TO ECUADOR

And your ears will hear a word behind you, saying, This is the way; walk in it, when you turn to the righthand and when you turn to the left.
— Isaiah 30:21

Our daughter, Ileana (Illy) was born our first year in Ecuador. We didn't know it, but Illy was going to need surgery that might not have been possible in Ecuador. We took our first Home Ministry Assignment (HMA) early so we wouldn't have to pay the extra for Illy to fly, which we would have done if we'd waited until the official date we were due for HMA. Looking back, I see that God's plan was for us to be back in Tasmania sooner, so that Illy could have the medical care she needed.

We were grateful to friends Mike and Annie for finding us a house to live in not far from their home. While that was one concern taken care of, and a major one, I wasn't prepared for the emotional roller coaster of being back in Tasmania, and I certainly wasn't prepared for the challenge of feeling lost, uncertain, and forgotten. Ross started back at work almost immediately, Miriam and Sarah left for school each morning, and I was … at home with Illy. I had no idea why I frequently found myself sitting on the floor, Illy in my arms, and crying while I rocked back and forth. During our second year at Bible College, I was diagnosed with depression, and took medication for a while, which did help. At the time, I thought it was just the stress of trying to keep up with studies and coping with the demands of community living; I never once considered it may be a spiritual issue and didn't even think to talk to God about it. After I had Miriam, I struggled for many months with feelings of despair and a deep sense of hopelessness that had me not wanting to get out of bed, resenting Miriam for being a colicky baby, and desperately wanting to understand what was happening to me. There were times when I would have taken my life if I had had the means. But I never mentioned this to Ross or to my mother-in-law who probably would have told me to just get on with things! Mum had a challenging life and was remarkably resilient. Sometimes when people are strong and able to cope well, they can't understand what it's like for those who don't. It isn't a deliberate desire to dismiss the reality of another, but a total inability to put themselves in another's place and therefore be able to offer comfort. Knowing what I do now, I am sure I had post-natal depression, and perhaps if I'd had the courage to talk to the Child Health Nurse, I would not have had to struggle for so long. As I look back at the times I have been so low, I can see God's grace at work protecting me from myself in many ways.

Although I talked very little about what was happening to me, my friends Anne and Annie, whom I mentioned earlier, seemed to know something wasn't quite right. Their friendship, I believe, played a significant part in keeping me safe in those first months back in Tasmania.

Home Ministry Assignment and Back to Ecuador

We hadn't been back long when we realised Illy, a little over eight months old, was very sick. She developed a raging temperature, and we did all we could that first night it occurred to bring it down. The next day we contacted our friend and GP, Trevor Clezy, as Illy was no better. He advised us to take her straight to the Emergency Department at the local hospital. It was a horrible experience. As soon as we mentioned Ecuador, it seemed the search was on for complex causes related to our time in the tropics. I couldn't bear to stay in the cubicle with tiny Illy screaming and sobbing as the doctors attempted to get blood from her. I was so glad Ross was there. Even after calling in the consultant, they sent us home none the wiser. After another night of dangerously high temperatures, I contacted Dr. Clezy again. He asked if they had taken a urine specimen at the hospital and I realised that, no, they hadn't. I slipped down to the surgery and picked up the necessary bag and prayed hard as I put it on Illy, knowing that it was often hit and miss the first couple of times trying to get a specimen from a baby. But it worked the first time—and it was full of protein, so much so that I would not have believed the specimen to be urine if I hadn't collected it myself. God's grace worked through Dr Clezy at that time, as he immediately ordered antibiotics for her that worked quickly to heal Illy of an infection that could have killed her.

It was a very busy time at home as we took Illy for tests which revealed that she had ureteric reflux, meaning that the urine would push back up into the kidneys—hence the serious infections. Then followed trips to a great paediatric urologist, a stay in Calvary in Hobart for surgery, and a very successful outcome. All this time we battled with whether we should go back to Ecuador or stay home. After much prayer and seeking the wise counsel of good friends, we returned to Ecuador in 1992, this time to Quito rather than Shell. Miriam and Sarah were in high school, and for various reasons, we knew it was time for us to move from Shell. We had stayed in Tasmania longer than anticipated because Ileana needed medical attention, but it was a good thing, because Ross and I really needed to know it was right for us to go back to Ecuador.

It was hard for us back in Quito. Ross was codirector of Medical Caravans and was away for a week at a time when they went out. Financial support seemed to be a constant problem, and I often wondered why, if God had called us there, he wasn't providing what we needed. And to top things off, Miriam was being very rebellious, and we were having problems with her at school and at home. It just seemed such a struggle.

We were visiting friends in Pifo, where the HCJB antennae farm was located, when Illy almost drowned. It was frightening to think we almost lost her again. But I was grateful and thanked God that He had allowed her to live. A few months later I collected Illy from kindergarten, and as we walked home, she was skipping and laughing, chatting to the dogs on the other side of some of the gates we passed. I was overwhelmed with love for her and for some reason found myself begging God, "Please, please, don't take her from me …"

The next day was Saturday. I yelled at Illy when she wouldn't stop pestering me, both Ross and I growling at her when she dropped rice all over the floor at lunch time, Miriam and Sarah sniped at each other, Ross did his thing, and I did mine. Later that day, I began preparing for dinner. There was a move at church to try to get people together who didn't know each other very well and we had offered to host a group. Miriam and Sarah were to babysit for one couple, but it did not surprise me when Miriam told Sarah she had asked a friend to go with her instead. So Sarah offered to bathe Ileana. I was in the kitchen, and Ross was at a practice for the Quito Day Concerts.

If … if … if … All the ifs in the world won't change things. However, if I had known Sarah planned to take a bath with Illy rather than supervising her in the bath, I wouldn't have allowed so much time to pass before checking on them. But … it is what it is, and I didn't know. As I worked in the kitchen, I didn't notice the smell of

Home Ministry Assignment and Back to Ecuador

gas. We had an Ecuadorian stove, and there was a slight gas leak from it, so we had it under a window and always kept the window open; I didn't notice the smell anymore. This evening while I stood there after putting something in the oven, I felt a sudden, very sharp pain right where my heart is—what I imagine it would feel like if someone stuck a knife in your chest and turned it. I gasped and had to bend forward a little, forcing myself to take deep breaths. It faded but left me perplexed—surely the gas leak wasn't that bad? Immediately after, I realised time was going and the girls would have to hurry, or everyone would arrive, and nothing would be ready; Sarah was going to set the table for me. She was excited about the evening, as she was the one who had encouraged us to host a group.

I walked out of the kitchen, and as I did, my heart began to pound. I knew fear and I could feel it breathing down my neck. Trying to shake it off, I called out to Sarah, but everything was quiet—too quiet; I felt as though I was in a fog as I walked to the bathroom. The door was closed, and there was no sound—nothing. I threw open the door, and it banged back against the vanity unit. Sarah's radio was on the unit, the bath was full, and there on the floor were my two girls. Illy was curled with her head towards me beside the bath; Sarah was between the vanity and the toilet—as though they had both become so tired, they just had laid down and gone to sleep. I screamed as I opened the window. I didn't know what to do first, but knew I needed help.

Our best friends, Steve and Eleanor, lived across the hall from us, and as I tore across there to bang so hard on the door I broke the doorjamb, I screamed, "My babies are dead—my babies are dead!" which brought Manuel, our concierge, racing up the stairs to see what was wrong. I was ahead of him though and sprinted back inside to start CPR while screaming at him to get our friends the Higginses from the third floor. What a horrible thing for a mother to have to do—decide which of her children to do CPR on first. I agonised over this later; guilt and condemnation sat on my shoulders for many years—I didn't want Sarah to think I loved her any less because I was working on Illy. But what sort of mother was I for this to have happened in the first place?

People came, things happened, someone went to get Ross, and next thing we were at Hospital Vozandes while a team worked on Illy and Sarah. Where is God when it hurts? I was wondering where he was through all of this and remembered He had said He would be with us. I trusted Him to keep His word, but it seemed to me He had let me down just like everyone else I trusted.

Ross was in with the team that was working on the girls. He became distressed when stomach contents came up while one doctor attempted cardiac compressions, so he took over. Occasionally, from the waiting room, we heard a machine beep. I held my breath, hoping it would continue. It didn't. The sounds stopped almost as quickly as they started and eventually those dreaded words, "There's nothing more we can do, I'm sorry." Where are you God in this?

They appeared to be asleep, and I didn't want to leave them. If God answers prayer, if He really loves us, then why were my girls lying still, lifeless, on cold hospital tables?

The following day, there was a memorial. As I think back, it was remarkable that in such a short time with so little notice, hundreds of people came from all over Ecuador. It truly was a time of coming together to comfort each other. I couldn't appreciate then all that went into making it happen and even the efficiency with which our return to Tasmania and the details of sending Illy and Sarah back were organised. All I could think was, *Why didn't God prompt me to go to the girls earlier? Why didn't He intervene? He could have. This didn't have to happen.*

I don't remember making a deliberate decision to turn my back on God and to cover my ears, but that's what I did. Yet despite this, there were times when I knew He was near, when I sensed His desire to comfort me. He was there when we walked from Finney's, the funeral parlour, to the gravesite, I sensed Him walking alongside, hand on my shoulder, and I knew He was there at WEC, the college that was

Home Ministry Assignment and Back to Ecuador

home to us before we went to Ecuador, where so many celebrated Illy's and Sarah's lives with us.

He was there too when I desperately called out for relief from the constant nightmares that took me back to that night and finding them in the bathroom. I longed for Holy Spirit to take away every memory of it, but He didn't. Instead, He replaced that horrific memory with a picture of Jesus standing between my smiling daughters, holding their hands. He wanted me to know He had been there with them.

Grief is a strange and very personal thing. Yet many of us who have experienced it can attest to similar experiences. Many a night I felt Ileana tugging on the side of the bed to pull herself up and then heave herself in between Ross and me. I'd wake with the sense of Ileana cuddled into me only to break into bitter sobbing as the hopelessness and desolation crashed over me again when I realised it was only a dream and I'd never again feel her warm little body in my arms. The pain wouldn't let up. The ache in my heart was fierce, and I cried so much I felt totally drained.

We went back to Ecuador after six weeks. It was necessary, if only for some sort of closure. We had left in such a hurry, and there was so much still to do. Neither of us sensed it was right to remain in Tasmania. There were those at home who wanted to know why we had come back at all; after all, God had called us to Ecuador, and we should have stayed regardless of what had happened. There were others who condemned us for wanting to return, and still others who loved us and cared for us unconditionally. Maurice and Jenny were always there for us, and their love helped us through that very hard time.

The lights of Quito were small specks when the crying and shaking began; it was impossible to stop. The flight attendant was very concerned, wanting to know what she could do. Ross reassured her that I would be OK, and finally we landed. As I walked off the plane, the dream I had before we left for Ecuador flashed into my mind, the one in which God had reassured me that He would be with us there, and I whispered, "So where were you?"

Driving into the garage of that same apartment building, I struggled to breathe. I didn't know what I felt, but I wasn't comfortable at all. Manuel, the porter, caretaker, and guard, was there to hug us both and warmly welcome us home. Steve and Eleanor had planned for us to stay with them while we organised our new apartment. They were, and still are, such good friends. While we were away, they cleaned out the old apartment and moved all our things to a smaller apartment at the back of the building on the third floor. There was no need for us to go back to the apartment where Illy and Sarah had died, and I was very grateful for that.

I learned quickly that friends and family have only so much patience for grief. Some expect those of us who are grieving to stand on our own two feet again from day one, even minute one. Some of our friends and family were more than willing to pull us from the mire of emotional quicksand, but they also expected us to make the effort and choices necessary for recovery. Only we could do that. So each morning, I made myself get out of bed, get dressed, and go to the compound. Although people asked how we were, I soon realised that most didn't want to know and were embarrassed if I was honest. I learned to smile when people said things like "You must be really special people for God to allow this to happen," or "God must have needed Ileana and Sarah more than you needed them here." Others would avoid me because they didn't know what to say, so I learned to politely say, "Fine. Thank you," when anyone asked how we were.

One day as I worked in the English language service, one missionary drew a chair up next to me and began peppering me with questions about that night, about what happened. It felt like an attack. Feeling very vulnerable and that I needed to protect myself, I hunched my shoulders and bowed my head as I tried to respond. I wanted to weep; the pain was so bad it was like a knife twisting in my gut and he just kept on until the tears poured down my face, then he said, "Good. You obviously have some feelings about what happened." He believed me to be unfeeling, uncaring, because I didn't cry all the time. Again,

Home Ministry Assignment and Back to Ecuador

it seemed we couldn't do the right thing. "Where are you God in all of this?" I wondered.

We remained in Ecuador for two and a half years. Miriam was a great concern for us and took most of our energy, as we attempted to deal with her rebellion. Finally, at the beginning of 1996, we decided we would take her out of school before she was expelled. By this time, we had moved to the HCJB Guest House as managers, and I continued with the English language service with radio programming while Ross continued to work with Medical Caravans.

Our plan was for Ross to take Miriam back to Tasmania, where she would finish years eleven and twelve while living with good friends. Everything was in place; Ross would remain in Tassie for six weeks, making sure Miriam was settled and spending time with his family.

I was in the Guest House office thinking about the next lot of paperwork I had to take care of, and Ross was outside doing something with the car. "Mum!" I looked up at the sharp tone in Miriam's voice. "I'm pregnant." Immediately, anger flooded me. "You stupid, stupid girl. Well, you can tell your father." I turned away from her. She was sixteen and thought she was madly in love with Fernando, her Ecuadorian boyfriend, who was five years older than her.

"What else, God? What have I done? Are you ever going to stop?" Angry words, questions I knew wouldn't be answered, but I asked them anyway. I couldn't believe Miriam would do this—she and Fernando deliberately planned for her to become pregnant so she wouldn't have to go back to Australia. They believed themselves in love and wanted to marry. I reminded Miriam of the many nights she had waited, in tears, for Fernando to pick her up while he had gone off partying with his friends without even letting her know he wasn't coming. I angrily reminded her of a lot of things, and there was very little love in my response to the whole situation.

Miriam adamantly refused to return to Australia, insisting she and Fernando wanted to marry. Fernando's parents came to see us. They loved Miriam and were their advocates. There was also a misunderstanding about our financial standing that had to be cleared up. Because we were expatriates living in Ecuador, they thought we were well off financially, as those who worked for various oil companies were, and there was an expectation that we would help support Miriam and Fernando.

Fernando Sr. and Cecilia are a lovely couple, and they were very gracious as we explained our situation to them. They left with the situation no clearer, as Miriam was still refusing to return to Tasmania with Ross. We spoke with Jim Allen, a caring and loving pastor and fellow missionary with HCJB, and he offered to do pre-marriage counselling for Miriam and Fernando if it came to that—and it seemed it would since Miriam was very stubborn, and we knew we couldn't drag her out of the country. But miracle of miracles, two nights before they were due to leave, Miriam was in her room downstairs and Ross and I were almost asleep when Miriam called out, "All right, I'll go, but I'm coming back as soon as I am 18!" What a relief!

In the midst of all this I had what I consider two supernatural experiences that were, in hindsight, God's way of showing that he was with me and loved me. These experiences happened before we moved from the old apartment building where we lived for a while after returning to Quito following the death of Ileana and Sarah, to the HCJB Guest House, which we managed until we finally returned to Tasmania for good. My sense of not being good enough coloured much of my thinking and understanding of God, so that without knowing it, I allowed my fear of not being admitted to heaven to become fears that God would refuse admittance to Illy and Sarah too—because they were my children.

I was in the lounge of the small apartment at the rear of the building. We had moved there on our return to Quito after Illy and Sarah died. I had walked from the bedroom, and one moment I was physically standing in the middle of the lounge, then next I knew I was in our old apartment, which was at the front of the building. I was standing near the window of Sarah's bedroom looking at her desk and wondering what I was going to do with her things when I heard the door open. I looked up, expecting it to be Ross, or perhaps Miriam, but it was Sarah. I must have looked shocked (I was!) because she said, "It's all right Mum."

I couldn't think, and the words that came were inane. "What are you doing here, SJ? Have you seen Grandma? Have you seen—"

"Don't ask questions, Mum," Sarah cut in softly but firmly. "I can't stay long. I've been allowed to come to tell you we're OK. We're happy, very happy, and you don't have to worry."

Her smile was a big Sarah smile. And before I could say anymore, she turned and left, gently closing the door behind her. And I was back in the lounge room with tears coursing down my face and a sense of peace and hope—just a spark. But it was there.

Some weeks later, I was resting on the couch in the lounge room. I was tired a lot of the time and sometimes in the afternoon would stretch out on the sofa for a while. It was midafternoon, and as I lay there with my eyes closed thinking about what to do for dinner, I felt the couch give a little as it does when someone sits down next to you. I knew I was alone in the apartment and dismissed it as my imagination. Then I felt a small hand touch my arm, "Mum, Mum, wake up!"

My eyes flew open at the sound of Illy's voice, and there she was, grinning at me. I quickly sat up, and she hopped on my lap, put her little arms around me and said, "Don't be sad mum, Sarah and I are happy. We love being with Jesus." She gently patted my cheeks, gave me a hug—and was gone.

I didn't speak of this to anyone for many years, thinking people would consider I had totally lost the plot, or even that I was dabbling in the occult. I understand that when a person is grieving, it is not unusual to have experiences where the presence of the deceased person seems very real. I'm sure there will be some who discount my experiences as grief-induced metaphysical events, and I accept that. However, I am convinced that it was a gift from a loving Father to a suffering daughter, even though I could not comprehend it as that at the time.

Sarah and I had just begun to get to know each other when she died. She and I walked in the mornings, and Sarah would ask me questions about spiritual things—I tried to answer as best I could but often felt out of my depth. One conversation we had was to have great significance for me some years later:

"What will we do in heaven?"

"I don't know really. Sing maybe."

"Well, if all we do is sing it will be pretty boring!"

Try this:

Have you ever thought, God can't possibly love me, otherwise he wouldn't allow all this stuff to happen to me? Write about that time. What was happening?

Even if we do not want to hear from God, He doesn't give up on us and will continue speaking, trying to get our attention, because He loves us. If you can remember a time when that happened to you, write about it. What did He say?

PAIN

> Mental pain is less dramatic than physical pain, but it is more common and also harder to bear. The frequent attempt to conceal mental pain increases the burden: it is easier to say 'My tooth is aching' than to say 'My heart is broken'.
> **— C. S. Lewis, The Problem of Pain**

I loved to play hide-and-seek when I was little and living with Grandma and Grandpa in Williamsford. A group of us would run off and hide, and one person would have to find us. One time, I found an excellent spot behind some shrubs and right under a wild blueberry bush. It was so comfortable there that I fell asleep and when I woke it was dark. I knew I was in trouble when I crawled out of my hidey-hole and found several people walking around with torches, calling my name. Despite Grandma's relief that I was OK, I didn't escape the tongue lashing and was banned from playing my favourite game again! I had found such a good hiding place that nobody could find me. I had, in a sense, closed myself off behind the shrubs and bushes and the only way they could find me was if I revealed myself.

Looking Back Moving Forward

Years later, God showed me that I closed much of myself off from Him in just the way I had hidden myself away during that game. I had heard often enough of the need to open all the rooms within myself so that Jesus could inhabit all of me, and to some degree I thought I had done that. Little did I know that there were places closed off that even I was not aware of. After Ileana and Sarah died, I thought time would eventually heal the wounds, that knowing that they were both safe with Him and being thankful to God because He showed me this, was enough, and eventually it would be OK. But it wasn't OK and wouldn't be until I faced the pain and the emotions associated with what had happened in Ecuador, and not only faced them but allowed myself to lean into, and push through them.

Just a few weeks after Illy and Sarah died, Ross and I were talking with someone who was going through a really difficult time. She was sharing her story and began to say how painful it was when she stopped suddenly, put her hand to her mouth and blurted, "I'm so sorry. How could I even say that? What I've been going through is nothing compared to what you've been through. The pain I feel must be so minimal."

I remember stopping her and saying, "Your pain is your pain. There are no degrees of pain, and no one can say that someone else's pain is worse than theirs." A similar scenario has played out many times over the years; someone in pain feels the need to play it down or brush it aside *saying,* "It doesn't compare to yours."

Well known Christian author and apologist C. S. Lewis called pain God's megaphone, and for good reason. God gets our attention instantly and fully when we are in pain—whether it be physical or emotional. Pain can also be our megaphone—the time when we shout loudly back to Him, "Why God? Why are you allowing this to happen to me?" And when we are so lost in the pain that we are unable to hear a response we shout more questions, "Don't you even care?"

When Jesus hung on the Cross, in the final moments of His life, blood loss began to draw away His strength, and asphyxiation His very breath. In the midst of horrific pain, physical and emotional as well as spiritual, Jesus shouted, *"Eloi, Eloi, lama sabacthani?"* "My God, my God, why have you forsaken me?"

I've thought about this. Was it an indication of self-doubt? Was Jesus doubting all that He knew to be true—His identity and mission? I don't believe so. I think this was when God intentionally entered our pain and misery. I can't possibly understand the reason behind everything that happens, everything God allows, but what I read in the Bible, in the account of the passion of Jesus, is that even when I can't see God working, He is, and I can trust His motives. God, who is in control of all things, who acts behind the scenes in all things, is also the God who willingly suffers. He can sympathise with those of us who suffer because He has experienced pain firsthand. I can shout at Him, cry with Him and find comfort in Him—if I will.

I don't remember a lot about the day of the memorial service for Illy and Sarah, but I do remember that while people filed into the Alliance Academy auditorium—the same place where hours before, many people joined together to pray that God would spare Illy and Sarah—I clutched Sarah's teddy bear tightly to me and asked no one in particular, "Why didn't God save them? He could have." And in my heart, I was saying, "My God, my God, why have you forsaken me?" There was no sense of His presence, His comfort. Words that were an attempt to comfort us, spoken by those who loved us, hurt rather than helped, seemed condemning rather than encouraging. I think it was then that doubt about God's love for me made its presence felt. I say this because God revealed to me many years later that doubt was always there; I just didn't acknowledge it. I was doing the ostrich trick and burying my head in the sand, hoping that the threat would disappear if I didn't acknowledge it.

One thing I do remember about that day is sitting in the auditorium, in the front row. At one stage, my gaze was drawn to the rafters. I can see it now as I write this—the face of Jesus with a look of such love and compassion that I felt it touch me. I saw this; I acknowledged it and I knew He was saying, "I have not forsaken you. Even in this I am with you." This was such a contrast to what had been before—that sense of abandonment, even rejection—yet doubt remained, and I'm sorry to say, it was doubt that won the battle that day.

The pain I speak of here is pain associated with loss. What I've found is that people attempt to categorise loss, to have a hierarchy of losses so that one is considered worse than another. But is it really possible to do this?

Pain, suffering, misery, tragedy. All of this is present every day. There is so much of it that at times it is overwhelming. We receive news from Barnabas Fund on a regular basis—just one group that highlights suffering on an immense scale through stories of real people being persecuted because they are Christians. We hear stories on the news about suffering closer to home, and I hear stories from clients about horrific suffering and pain. My awareness and ability to have compassion for others who are suffering, and to empathise with them, is heightened by my own experience and the confidence of hearing God say, "You can do that. You can help others to healing and freedom using your own experiences."

I have come to see that no matter the kind of loss experienced, it is horrible. We can't quantify and compare, because when we try to do this, it makes things worse. Those who feel their loss and pain aren't significant enough are deprived of the validation they need to experience the loss for the awful thing it is. They begin to feel guilty for the depth of their suffering over something they perceive as of little significance because they are told, "There are others worse off," and, "You should just get over it." Those who have suffered "big" losses may then believe that they, and only they, have suffered, and because of this no one can ever understand. So they drift forever in a no-man's-land where there is no lasting help. Being a Christian doesn't make you immune to this; in fact, Christians, as much as anyone else, can become victims of their loss and indulge themselves with the pain, eventually allowing this loss and pain to define who they are. There is

Pain

a danger that someone who is a Christian will decide that what they have believed can't be true because a God who loves them would not allow them to suffer, and so they turn their back on God. I know because I did just that.

There is something about being a missionary that causes you to wear a mask. Or perhaps it was just me. Before we left for Ecuador, we met many new people, we spoke at lots of meetings, and inevitably there was someone who said, "You're so brave, it's wonderful what you are doing. I could never do that." Those words pop into your mind when you least expect or want them. I built them into a demand, an expectation that I had to live up to. This left me in a vulnerable place, because as I saw it, if I shared what was really happening, how I truly felt, I would let many down. I had to be always on top of things, spiritually mature to the extent that my faith was always seen to be strong and able to withstand the hardest blows. So the mask was always there for me to slip on, to ensure the real me, the disappointing me, wouldn't be seen.

Recently, while back in Ecuador, I had some time with a friend from our early days there. It was time for their family to leave for Home Ministry Assignment—what used to be known as furlough. He was struggling in the same way I had. How do you be honest with your supporters? How can you share your doubts, your concerns? How can you possibly be real, knowing you'll most likely lose support, particularly financial support, because without it, it isn't possible to continue as a missionary? How do you share the uncertainty about whether you are still where God wants you? You can't ask them to pray with you knowing there will be those who disdain that uncertainty, that vulnerability, and will choose to withdraw their support because you just don't measure up in their eyes.

When Illy and Sarah died, and possibly even when Mum died, without realising it, I put on the mask again. The shock initially dulls everything; there is a numbing quality to it that wraps around you like a protective shell. But then the impact hits with force and there aren't words adequate to describe it, although we do try with words like *torment, affliction, horror, agony, suffering, distress, heartache, and misery.* But how can you describe what is happening emotionally, mentally, physically? The dream I had while at WEC, of being in a deep, black pit with a vicious, constantly spinning whirlwind threatening to drag me into itself is as close as I can get, yet even that is lacking. Just as it was almost impossible in that dream to stand against the power of the whirlwind, it was impossible to confront the anguish. The pain I experienced that moment in the kitchen when it felt like someone had pierced my heart with a dagger, remained. Unwelcome guest that it was, it stayed. No medications, no cream or ointment, no massage therapy could ease the pain. It dogged me, persistent in its presence, yet hidden so only I was aware of it—sometimes sharp and almost debilitating, sometimes a dull ache, but always there.

We have a wood fire at home, and it is necessary to have a supply of wood on hand. As limbs fall from the many trees on our block, Ross finds the time to cut them up and stack the wood into neat, easily accessible piles. To make the chopping easier he hired a log splitter to deal with the extra big pieces, breaking them down into sizes he can stack as they are, or easily split into smaller pieces with the axe. I'm not fond of heavy machinery, but one day I felt I should offer to help Ross as he had a lot of wood to get through and only had the log splitter for the day. I was feeling confident enough to place the wood on the machine and push it through, but I lost concentration for mere seconds and forgot to lift the lever before attempting to take the log from the machine. My left hand was caught between the log and the steel plate that prevented it from being pushed off the machine; twenty-five tonnes of pressure used to split great, thick logs, pressed down on my fingers. Initially, the shock was so great, I felt nothing. Then the pain hit me, and I was too afraid to look at the damage. The nerves screamed at me to do something to mitigate or eliminate the pain.

Our bodies are designed to communicate pain; it is a protective mechanism that warns us something is wrong. What is true in the

Pain

body is true in our soul. When we lose something precious, something terribly important to us, the screaming pain we feel reflects the value of what is lost. We respond to pain in different ways. I did fight it, but I think our eldest daughter Miriam's rebellion, which I may well have used as an excuse, also complicated things. While our focus was on Miriam, I didn't have to face the pain. But in doing that, I didn't allow myself to grieve either. I pushed my emotions away into a hidden place inside me and hoped they would fall asleep as I had under that wild blueberry bush when I was a child. It was much easier to deny the pain, to hide it away, keep it silenced, and go about everything as though nothing had happened. It seemed much better to do this when people were obviously uncomfortable around me, and when other things demanded attention. When people asked, "How are you?" I said, "Fine. Thank you." It was a relief for them and a relief for me as well.

When we returned to Ecuador after our short time back in Tasmania, we were in a different apartment. I had photos dotted around and sometimes I would look at them and find myself standing there with tears rolling down my face, the pain pushing its way to the surface. Paula, a lovely Quichua lady who helped in the house, became distressed when she saw me cry and insisted I should put away everything that reminded me of Illy and Sarah and not think about them. And, although I did not agree with her, I found myself doing just that. I couldn't look at photos or watch videos—it was too hard. Jerry Sittser in *A Grace Disguised* says that denial puts off what we should face. He's right. In denial we refuse to see the loss for what it is, something terrible that can't be reversed. It took several years for Miriam to go to Carr Villa, the cemetery where Illy and Sarah are buried. When I asked if she had been, her response was, "No. If I don't go, I can still imagine that one day they will walk through the door again."

I teach people about grief and loss now, among other things. When I talk about grief and loss, I am clear about the need to confront pain, rather than dancing around it with eyes lowered. Choosing not to confront the pain is, in a sense, not dealing with it at all, and we lose when we choose this path. Writer Frederick Buechner says that "even the saddest things can become, once we make peace with them, a source of wisdom and strength for the journey that lies ahead." But *we* choose whether to make peace with them. In the end, it doesn't matter what we do to try to deflect pain, the unrelenting nature of it means it will catch us, it will have that showdown.

I had been a Christian for many years before the accident, a missionary for only a few, but it is only since the accident that God has become a living reality to me. My confidence in God is quieter but stronger. I feel little pressure to impress God or prove myself to Him; yet I want to serve Him with all my heart and strength. Over the years of trying to hide from Him and allowing doubt and fear to dominate my life, He was teaching me where He belongs, at the centre of my life, not on the edges. Thirteen years after Illy and Sarah died, I finally allowed God to assume that place. It was only after I allowed God to assume His rightful place in my life that He was able to show me there was more to my refusal to acknowledge the pain that was so much a part of Illy and Sarah dying. I wasn't aware of the silent pain that I had carried for many years, the silent pain that was behind the way I often responded to things that happened in my life. How could I talk about what it meant to me to be rejected by my mother and my father when I didn't understand it myself?

Mum and I were having a rare moment of togetherness in the kitchen when I asked her why she left Dad. "I married him because I wanted two children. So when I had you and your sister, I left." I'm not sure what I hoped to hear, but this response was not it. There was no love between my parents; in fact, from what Mum said, she had manipulated Dad to get something she wanted. And yet once she had her two children, she quickly dropped us with willing, or unwilling, relatives and went off to live her life, a life that did not have room for children.

Pain

Dad—well, Dad was very much a self-interested person, a man whose mother spoiled him as he grew, so that he believed he was the centre of everyone's universe. Despite his father's hard-line religious stand, Dad was, as much as possible, sheltered by his mother and came to rely on her protection. His parents frowned on his marriage to Mum, but because he was the golden boy, they grudgingly agreed to it. However, because of the attachment to his mother, it was hard for him to "leave both mother and father and cleave to his wife."

I knew all this, and I thought I had left it behind. But when God began to draw me out of the hiding place that I thought no one knew about, He showed me not only that there was a lot I needed to work through in relation to the death of Illy and Sarah, but that there was more—what I had not wanted to face about my growing-up years.

In her book, *Silent Pain*, Kathy Olsen says that it isn't the painful emotional events of our lives that cause the lingering emotional distress, rather it is the silence about those events and the feelings associated with them that is so damaging. I work with several people who struggle with false guilt. False guilt causes us to remain silent; to push pain down and pretend it isn't there, usually because we blame ourselves for what happened to cause the pain. False guilt is based on self-condemning feelings that we haven't lived up to expectations—our own or someone else's. We blame ourselves even though we have committed no wrong, or if we have done something wrong, we continue to blame ourselves even after we are forgiven. And false guilt keeps us in bondage to shame, fear, and anger. All three were my constant companions.

The worst thing about false guilt is that confession does not resolve it—there is no sin. I blamed myself for Illy and Sarah dying; I knew it was because I was a terrible mother that they had died, that God had taken them. But this was a lie that took so long for me to recognise. Revelation 12:10 says that Satan is the accuser of the brethren (of those who belong to God). He enjoys burdening us with false guilt and condemnation, and his favourite strategies are bringing up the past, reminding us of our failures, and making us feel unforgiven and unaccepted by God. So, I accepted that it was my fault Mum and Dad didn't want me. I accepted that there must be something wrong with me. It was my fault that so many horrible things happened to me as I grew up; it was my fault Illy and Sarah died; it was my fault Miriam, our remaining daughter, was so rebellious … I failed, failed, failed. Those were the words hammering away at me constantly.

After a while, the guilt changes to shame. Shame and guilt are close relatives—not the same, but very close. Shame, says June Hunt, "is a painful emotion of disgrace caused by a strong sense of guilt." Shame kicks in when guilt moves from knowing you have done something bad to feeling that you are bad. Shame is not just about what you have or have not done but about who you are. I was so ashamed of who I was; I was from the wrong side of the tracks, so to speak, with alcoholism and failed relationships littering the family history from as far back as I knew. That I had started down that road too before I was saved was cause for shame. That was my identity, and I believed I was basically defective, which lead to a deep sense of unworthiness and a constant fear of abandonment and rejection.

Is it any wonder then that fear had such a powerful hold on me? Fear and shame both stem from harsh parental discipline and degrading attitudes. Fears can float around unnoticed, but wherever there is false guilt, there are the fears as well, because they are a by-product of allowing false guilt to have a hold over you. Whenever we feel the pain of shame, we also feel fear of rejection, fear of punishment, and fear of isolation, and out of this comes the belief that we are worthless.

Living with the fear of worthlessness, rejection, or loneliness eventually leads to developing a fear-based personality, one that is buried deep in the roots of childhood shame and can stay with you for all of your life. As an adult, I wore the outer clothes of success. I did well at most things. I appeared confident and strong, but underneath I was afraid people would see the real me, the needy me, so I hid who

Pain

I really was. This is dishonesty, and living a lie completely undermines the likelihood of love and intimacy in close relationships.

As a way of dealing with this, I became angry, because anger is a natural way of fighting guilty feelings. Guilt contacts your emotional antennae and sends out messages of shame. When you feel shame that you have done something wrong, the threat of rejection surfaces, and anger becomes the weapon of choice to use against the person who exposes your fault or the significant person who sees your inadequacies and may expose you, or the hurting person longing for acceptance (you). Yes, the anger can be turned on yourself. A lovely lady I was speaking to recently said that she slaps herself on the face, hard, when she realises she said something she shouldn't have said, something she wishes she could take back but can't—something she feels guilty about. I came to dislike and almost hate myself for not living up to the expectations of those who are important to me, for being inferior. For many years I compared myself with my husband and always found myself wanting. I constantly felt that I did not measure up, especially to the expectations Ross's parents had for the woman he married. When Illy and Sarah died, I added to the silent pain of many years the false guilt and the shame that came from not being able to take care of my children. After they died, fear intensified its attack so that I lived in its shadow, always waiting for the next punishment—who would God take from me next?

The freedom I found through the VMTC ministry, where God could minister to me and break me out of my prison, gave me the courage and confidence to stand up and share my story at Gateway Baptist Church one Sunday morning in 2009. It was the first time I shared, publicly, how hard it was for me after Illy and Sarah died. Pastor Steve asked me to share how my faith had sustained me through challenges and difficulties and how I had managed to keep walking, keep moving forward spiritually. Instead, I shared the struggles and the desire to keep the struggles hidden, the need to pretend I was someone I wasn't. For the first time, I was open and honest and allowed myself to be vulnerable. And, as I shared, I knew that all those hidden things were now revealed. The light of Truth totally eclipsed the darkness surrounding them. And that meant that guilt, shame, fear, and anger were no longer strongholds in my life. The real me was emerging!

Try this:

Are you in a place where pain is destroying you, yet you feel unable to share what is happening with anyone? If so, write about it and then talk with God about what you write.

Have you experienced God's peace in the midst of deep pain? If so, write about what that was, or is, like for you.

TRUST

> Lean on, trust in, and be confident in the Lord with all your heart and mind and do not rely on your own insight or understanding. In all your ways know, recognise, and acknowledge Him and He will direct and make straight and plain your paths.
>
> **— Proverbs 3:5-6**

Trust was a word I was familiar with by the time we left for Ecuador. God gave the above verses to both Ross and me, and I knew the word and the verses well and happily shared them at every opportunity.

I thought if I repeated the verses often enough, trust would become real to me. But I was building on an unstable foundation. Trust is a matter of the heart. If we don't trust, we depend on our own logic and ways of understanding, which are mostly a product of our world environment.

Trust is essential in any relationship and research shows that most marriages break down because trust is broken or does not exist. Mum and Dad divorced when I was eighteen months old and my sister, Kim, was three and a half. Neither trusted the other, and each was intent on doing what seemed good without consideration for the other. From early days this became the pattern, with neither of them recognising how destructive their behaviour was. They were depending on their own logic and ways of understanding to build their marriage, but this wasn't a solid foundation, so their marriage simply crumbled.

Similarly, I was trying to build my Christian life on an unstable foundation. The foundation I was building on was what I knew about God, what I had learned through others who had input into my life, and what I learned through study at WEC. Trust couldn't be a part of my life because it is a very personal thing and is a heart relationship with God. You can't learn it from a book or from someone else. Because of this, doubt and uncertainty were always lurking close by. The doubt, which I didn't recognise, was rooted in my understanding of people who had been a part of my life before I came to know Jesus, and in my past experiences. Doubt leads to unbelief; trust and unbelief cannot co-exist. However, trust and faith are inextricably linked, they can't be separated. You must believe and have faith in someone before you can trust them. Every child should be able to trust his or her parents. Often, our relationship with our parents is what we try to mimic in our relationship with God.

I was about ten when I finally understood that Mum had a serious drinking problem. I was fossicking through the dirty clothes basket one day looking for an item of clothing that I wanted urgently when I found a half-full bottle of sherry. It seemed strange that a bottle of sherry would be in amongst the dirty clothes, so I pulled it out and took it to Mum, thinking innocently that she had accidentally put it there. While she wasn't happy with me and quickly snatched the bottle from me, I accepted that it was just one of those things. Sometime later, I dropped an earring behind mum's dressing table, and when I leaned over to rescue it, I found not one, but two bottles of sherry, one half full and the other completely full. I didn't pull them out though, because as I looked at them, I remembered that the day before when I arrived home from school, Mum had been in the

Trust

chair in the lounge room, not even dressed, hair still in curlers and she hadn't even spoken to me when I banged into the house. John had prepared tea for us that night.

After that, I was aware that things weren't as they should be, and I often caught Mum out lying to me about something. In my high school years, I was frequently embarrassed when the nuns pulled me aside and told me that I would have to speak to Mum about paying the school fees. The first time I had such an interview, I did speak to Mum, and she was so furious with me, saying that of course she had paid them, that I really didn't want to have to mention it again. After that, I dreaded the talk from well-meaning nuns who didn't want to send the debt collector to the door. It was the same with other things. Mum would promise me she had paid the bills, that she had done what she said she would do, but I learned not to trust her. I had no faith in any of her promises because she never carried them through. She did not honour her word. I took part in eisteddfods, in school plays, in sporting events—for a while. When Mum consistently said she would attend but rarely did, I just stopped participating. I couldn't trust her.

It was the same with Mum's drinking. I had no understanding of what it meant to be an alcoholic and I wanted her to stop drinking because I didn't like her when she was drunk. She would say things that were very hurtful or become extremely melancholy and weepy, or she would simply not talk at all. So, thinking I was helping, I began searching for the bottles and when I found them, I would tip the contents down the sink. This caused Mum to be horribly angry with me and eventually I realised that as fast as I got rid of the bottles, Mum would replace them. We didn't have a car, but the local taxi could probably have driven to our place without a driver. I refused to answer the door when the driver knocked, knowing it would be another bottle in the brown paper bag he carried.

Other adults in my life, who were supposed to be trustworthy destroyed that trust. I believe, though, that my relationship with Mum and Dad was the most significant in my unconscious decision not to trust—or to demand a lot of proof before I would place my trust in anyone again. I was always expecting to be deceived, that the person asking me to trust them would fail me, and many times I was right.

Because I was expecting to be deceived, I gave deception rights over my life. I did the same with doubt and fear. It was doubt that whispered to me, "Are you really saved? Does God really love you?" And of course, fear joined in, "When you die, you'll get to heaven and God will tell you that you can't enter. You're not good enough. He never intended for you to be saved. You just think you are." Anger wasn't far behind. I didn't know how to deal with doubt and fear and the uncertainty that dogged me, so I lashed out in anger, or withdrew just as I had as a child. I hid this from most people, but Ross and the girls bore the brunt of it. And this would come back to haunt me after Ileana and Sarah died.

Our time in Ecuador was meant to be a time when we would do great things for God. We were full of zeal and sure we would win souls wherever we went. It wasn't like that. I was to remember later the words of Don Barns, one of our lecturers at College: "God doesn't take you anywhere for what you can do for Him. He takes you where he can best work on and in you."

What I didn't realise was that God calling us to Ecuador was part of His plan for us—part of Him drawing us into a loving, transforming, forgiving, empowering relationship with Him. He wanted us to draw into intimacy with Him, to teach us what it is to walk in the Spirit and to live out of a place of peace and rest instead of striving all the time to do what we thought was right and good. But here again, I continued to live and minister out of my own ways of understanding and logic.

I was such a Martha, and I was very good at telling God what I was going to do and how I would do it. It was important to me to have the acceptance of those back home who were supporting us, and also to be liked and accepted by our fellow missionaries. To achieve this, I had to be busy all the time, making sure I had news to tell when I wrote home and that I didn't give anyone in the mission reason to say I was slack. It was also important for me, for my sense of self-worth, to be seen to be competently achieving in some way. I was selfish and self-centred and had no idea this was the case. I believed I was doing good things for God. And I was definitely trusting in my own abilities, because I did not understand what it meant to be Spirit lead.

Ross and I both have strong regrets about how our selfishness resulted in us missing out on precious time with our children. We know we are forgiven, but even so, we are aware of how different things might have been. Ross is a musician and loves to spend time writing and recording and playing music. He recalls with sorrow how he would lock himself away, ignoring Ileana, who knocked and called out to him, wanting to spend time with her daddy. And I recall being eager to dash off to my work with the mission; after all, that's why we were there.

After Illy and Sarah died and we came back to Australia, my lack of trust in God lead me to throw myself into my nursing career. We had been back almost a year, had moved into our new home, and I was walking to the letter box one day when I heard very clearly, "What are you doing and why are you doing it?" I acknowledged the words, but didn't dwell on them or think about them, because it would have opened up a Pandora's box for me. I might have stopped running a little sooner if I had taken time then to think about what I was doing and why. Over the years I heard those words at times, and for a moment I would stop—but only for a moment. I would even laughingly comment on them when we were with others, but I didn't take them seriously, because that would have meant not only facing my pain but also acknowledging that I was running from God. God graciously persevered with me, waiting for me to be ready to face Him again. I am reminded of the Scripture that tells me God is faithful; He is always with me and will never leave me or forsake me (Hebrews 13:5). Once we are His, no one can snatch us out of His hand (John 10:30).

I've learned that when God teaches us lessons, He wants us to teach them to others. One of those is that we need to regularly stop and think about our priorities and ask ourselves *that* question, "What am I doing and why am I doing it?" We were settling back into life in Tasmania, and I was working at a local hospital when I had an opportunity to share the priorities lesson with a colleague. That day one of the nurses I worked with looked distracted; it was around mid-morning, and we were in the treatment room getting medications ready for our patients. I asked if she was OK, and she told me she had received a call from her son's school. Her son was sick and was asking for her, but she felt she should stay at work because she was needed there. I wasn't in the habit of sharing about Illy and Sarah, but felt I needed to then. The nurse was shocked but thanked me and said it helped her see things in perspective. I'm happy to say she went to be with her son.

In a world that has lost its understanding of the word *trust*, we are on guard immediately when someone says, "Trust me." It's easy to allow this reservation to slip into our relationship with God. We tend to put him in a human box and expect that He will act and respond as we might. So to "trust in the Lord with all of your heart" is easy to say but not so easy to do. When things don't go as we want them to, we think, *I told you so.* The next time God says, "Trust Me," we stand back and ask, "Why should I?"

We receive lots of great supernatural gifts when we come into a relationship with Jesus. One of those is faith. God's call to us is to live by faith alone, and Rick Joyner says it is the nature of God's call to separate us from all we have known and built our lives on. It is faith that enables us to believe that God loves us and has a good plan for us, and it also enables us to trust that God will do what He has promised. When we start out on our journey with God, we have everything in seed form. Jesus is the seed of everything good: and like any seed, it will only grow if we nurture it. The ground the seed is in must be cultivated and weeded—our lives and hearts are the ground for what God has planted in us, and in order for the seed to grow, we must allow God, through Holy Spirit, to work in us to bring about the necessary change. This is ongoing and does not happen overnight. Faith grows as we nurture it, as we pull out and destroy weeds such as fear and doubt, that tend to choke the growing faith.

Faith, according to Colossians 1:4 and 2:5, is "leaning of the entire personality on Him in absolute trust and confidence in His power, wisdom and goodness." Holy Spirit is the one who grows our faith as He teaches and guides us through the Word of God and through others He brings into our lives. As faith grows through seeing God at work, through good teaching, and through our own growing relationship with God, we begin to see that life is far more than what this world offers. It is difficult for us to see with spiritual eyes until we learn to walk in the Spirit, but as we do, our focus shifts from here to eternity.

One of my clients told me that she sees God and knows His presence in a way that is as real as my presence with her. She has only recently come to know God in this way. Before she could come to this, we worked together to weed out those things that were stopping her from growing, to clear away the useless shrubbery that was keeping the path forward hidden. She began to understand what it means to be raised with Christ and to set her mind on what is above rather than the things that are on the earth. Her faith grew exponentially as she opened herself up to God and cleared away the obstacles that prevented her from seeing who she is in Christ and from seeing God as a loving father—a loving father who has a good plan for her life and who has, through Jesus, given her right standing with Him and peace and joy in Holy Spirit. Now she is ready for God to grow the seed of trust because the ground is prepared, and the seed is already sprouting.

I think of those verses from Proverbs God gave to Ross and me and shake my head. If we had truly understood them, what He was saying to us, I wonder what things might have been like. But then it's no use thinking that way. I can see that God has and is and will continue to separate us from things or people we try to build our lives on; that is a function of the nature of His call. Much as I kick a little sometimes, I accede to His greater wisdom these days. I'm only glad now that when I read the Word, Holy Spirit brings revelation, so I am not likely to miss what He wants me to understand and apply. I ask Him for revelation rather than depending on others; after all, He has made it clear that we can hear His voice. All of us who are His can hear His voice—we just have to take the time to listen. I am conscious, however, of the wisdom of God at work in His people and enjoy talking about the Word and what God is saying to me through it, which in turn opens up ways for Him to bring further revelation through people I know I can trust.

Returning to Ecuador in 2012 was a case of trusting God implicitly to work it all out. I did not want to go but accepted that He wanted me to return for some reason. Once I decided I would go, I wanted to plan and organise; God would not allow me to. He challenged my declaration of trusting Him: "You say you trust me, and you tell others you trust me, now let's test that …"

Try this:

Ask yourself, "What am I doing and why am I doing it?" Write down your answer. Talk to God about it.

Answer the following questions: *Who am I? Why am I here? What do I want?* Write, and then review your answers. Is there something that stands out for you? If so, what is it? What will you do about it?

LOOKING BACK MOVING FORWARD – RETURN TO ECUADOR

For I am about to do something new. See, I have already begun! Do you not see it?

— Isaiah 43:19

Late in 2011 as I walked my usual 4.5-kilometre route around a nearby crescent and lake, the words, *It's time for you to return to Ecuador,* passed through my mind. They were quite clear, clear enough that I responded out loud, *"No, I don't think so. Why would I do that?"* I mentioned it in my journal but didn't explore it any further. It made little sense for me to go back to Ecuador. As far as I was concerned, that part of our life was over—finished. We still had contact with some friends who remained in Ecuador and others no longer there, but only limited contact. It was easy for me to dismiss the thought.

Some weeks later, just before Christmas, once again as I walked around the block, the thought came strongly, *"It's time for you to go back to Ecuador."* This time I didn't dismiss it outright; I agreed that if this was God speaking to me, I would go—and then I forgot about it. Then, in January 2012, the words came again, and this time they were so clear I thought someone had walked up behind me and spoken to me. At that point I thought I would mention it to Ross. I knew it was I who had to go back to Ecuador, that I wasn't being told it was time for Ross and me to return. When I mentioned it, I was expecting Ross to dismiss the idea, and I was a bit taken aback when all he said was, *"Yes, I agree."* That threw me, particularly as his response was immediate; he didn't even have to think about it! It was then I decided I should at least think and pray seriously about the possibility of going back.

By this time, our grandson, Samuel, was back in Ecuador with his Ecuadorian family, so I thought it would be a good opportunity to see him and to get to know that side of his family better. When Samuel's grandparents kindly offered their home for me to stay with them, I tentatively made plans. I emailed some friends in Ecuador and mentioned on Facebook I would be returning. I was sure that if I was going, I should have an itinerary and plan for things to be in place. This is where things got tricky, and God really tested me.

I like to plan and organise things, to know what is happening, and it made sense to me that if I were to go all that way, I should make the most of it. But … I had a strong sense that God was saying, *"Don't plan, just go."* That just did not make sense to me, and I was sure God would want me to share with people back in Ecuador what He had done in my life. Hmm … a verse I learned well and used to say a lot in Spanish is, "El hombre pone, pero Dios dispone." It was one my Latin friends used often too. In English we would say, "We make our plans, but God is the one who has the final decision." Proverbs 16, verse 9 is well known, but I really don't think I had seen how relevant it is until that time—well, perhaps not so obviously anyway. Some of my friends said it would be nice to see me, but no one seriously committed to meeting with me. That did not sit well with me at all, so

Looking Back Moving Forward - Return to Ecuador

I continued trying to put things in place. At one point I said to God that I felt strongly that I should email a particular person who was a pastor and offer my services in counselling, speaking, or whatever might be helpful. The response I received was *"You can email but you won't hear back."* And I didn't hear back! Then it seemed someone wanted me to share my story and so I arranged to meet them, but that fell through as well. Every time I tried to organise things, whatever I was doing just did not happen—a case of "Karen pone, pero Dios dispone!" After all the effort I had put in with no success, I was on my way home from one of my walks when I heard, *"Will you just go?"* So, muttering and mumbling about not knowing what was going on, I gave in and booked flights to Ecuador, thinking that at least I had somewhere to stay. A few days later, Samuel's father contacted me and said it wouldn't be convenient for me to stay with his parents, as his father had just been diagnosed with lung cancer. I had flights booked but no idea where I would stay, who would pick me up from the airport or if I would do nothing but sit in one spot for the entire time I was there. This really was a trust test! In one of her teachings, Joyce Meyer tells how one day after she had decided nothing was working, she just sat down and cried out, *"I give up!"* to which Holy Spirit responded, *"Really? Thank goodness!"* I did much the same thing at this point and sensed Holy Spirit saying almost the same to me except I heard *"Finally!"* The day before I left Tasmania, I was talking with Samuel via Skype when his grandfather, Fernando Sr, came on to say *hello*. He told me they were expecting me and that I was, of course, welcome to stay with them. He had arranged for his son, Samuel's father, to meet me, and he would look forward to seeing me after he returned home from a chemotherapy session. Well! That was a relief; at least accommodation was sorted!

I was nervous as we left for the airport. People had been asking me if I was excited and if I was looking forward to the trip and my time away. But really, I wasn't, because I did not know why I was going or what I could expect once there.

The last time we had left for Ecuador, we had been home for just a few weeks. That time, we left without Illy and Sarah, whose bodies remained interred at Carr Villa Cemetery in Launceston. We left with the blessings of some and the recriminations of others ringing in our ears, and we left with a recalcitrant and sulky Miriam. I felt tears well up and my throat constrict as I remembered. Why, after all this time? I wondered. Why am I doing this?

This time was different—before there was no sense of God's presence, perhaps because I didn't want to acknowledge it; this time I knew He was with me. In an almost tangible, physical way, I felt Him holding my hand firmly, lovingly, as if to say, *"I know it's hard, but I am with you, as I have always been."* It was God and me. No doubts this time. The journey had begun—although as I thought about it, I realised that the journey commenced in September of 2011 when I said *yes*. To obey is better than sacrifice. Last time it was about sacrifice; this time it was about obedience.

The thought of the long flight concerned me, but we had a nice new plane with plenty of leg room and comfortable seats. Flight staff looked after us very well too. So that concern was taken care of. The next one was getting through LA International and finding my way to the next flight in time, as I had heard horrible stories about long delays and people missing their onward flights because of this. I took a deep breath and headed in to line up with everyone else, a bit daunted by all the people, as two other flights had arrived close to ours. I couldn't see any way to get through in time to catch the next flight and was talking to God about this when someone said, "You in this line—you come here. Hurry, you come …" Six of us headed off to the express lanes, and I was through that first part within half an hour of us landing. Ah, but then it was the luggage screening—those lines were longer still. Then: *"Do you have anything to declare?"*

"Well, no, except some chocolate biscuits."

Looking Back Moving Forward - Return to Ecuador

"Not Tim Tams—we'll have to confiscate those, ma'am!" He smiled widely. "Go on through ma'am, you have a good trip."

Off I went. I dropped off my suitcase, and after a bit of wandering and being rescued by a very pleasant airport employee, I ended up at the gate lounge just an hour after touching down from Australia! I could tell that this was special and knew God's presence in a tangible way, even in the conversations that opened up along the way. I slept on the flight to Miami, making me well rested when I finally boarded the plane for the four-hour Miami-Quito flight.

I looked for the lights as soon as the pilot told the cabin crew to prepare for landing. I pushed up the shade expecting … I don't know, but dense cloud shrouded the plane and only darkness stared back at me. I tugged down the shade and leaned back, taking a deep breath, and letting it out again with a sigh of relief.

"Trust me. Let the memories come. Lift the shade."

So I did. I lifted the shade and light was all around. Strings and trails of brilliant orange, sometimes white, stretched across the plateau, down into the valley and up into the distant hills. I gasped then glanced quickly at the young woman sitting next to me, but she slept on.

"Let the memories come."

I turned back to the narrow pane of glass, gaze fixed on flickering lights, but my mind was busy as memories of another flight into Quito chased each other through it.

When I noticed I was holding my breath, I carefully let it out, watching the window fog as I did. Tension I hadn't been aware of dissipated like the moisture on the window. I leaned my forehead against the cold glass. It was OK.

We landed safely and softly in the middle of Quito. There was no clapping, so I assumed the pilots had plenty of practice these days and a safe landing wasn't unusual enough to warrant applause. Before long, we were exiting the plane via a walkway that hadn't been there last time. It took us into the customs and immigration area, which was much the same. It was here for some reason that I felt anxious. But not for long—a plane from Santiago, Chile, had just landed, so there were lots of people attempting to get through the necessary officialdom. The Latin people are very comfortable moving through lines and slipping in ahead of others. I had forgotten what it is like to have so many people with so much luggage (carry-on items that would have our airlines in fits) trying to squeeze through a space meant for about a third that many. Ankles and toes are fair game. And it doesn't matter how severe the injury or how many times one is run over or into, a *disculpe* or *excuse me* is considered a sufficient apology. I laughed to myself even as I asked, *"What am I doing here? What is the point of this?"*

"Just go."

I had gone, was there, and so I kept moving, dodging trolleys and suitcases coming from all directions.

A voice from behind startled me out of my reverie. *"Is this the line for foreigners?"* they asked in Spanish. And I was pleasantly surprised that I responded automatically—in Spanish! From the moment we arrived in Los Angeles I was hearing as much Spanish as English, but until now I hadn't needed to speak it. The young woman checking our documents asked me in laboured English if I was in Ecuador for a holiday. I responded in English, and the blank look on her face caused me to switch to Spanish. She became animated, and we had a quick and lively conversation for that time of night. It encouraged me. I hadn't spoken Spanish for fifteen years and was not too sure how I would go, but I felt it coming back and thought I would be able to at least make myself understood. If I had known then what God had planned for me as far as using Spanish, I might have taken the next flight out of Quito rather than exit the airport!

Memories were coming quickly and in waves: the very first time we arrived in Ecuador; when we returned from HMA after Illy had been so unwell; and, of course, the last time when we were a family of three and not five. Even the luggage collection area brought back memories. No courtesy here! They threw the luggage from our flight and the Air Chile flight on the floor just past the immigration booth. It was a case of everyone for himself as people spotted their luggage and hopped and leaped over other bags to grab their own, heaving it back over the top of the pile to toss it onto a trolley or even across the room. Cries of *"Ow!"* mingled with *"Perdone"* and *"Disculpe"* as more toes were squashed, and ankles and shins scraped. Phew! I saw mine right in the middle. So over I went, navigating around the bags and avoiding other people and made it back to the customs line with minimal damage to myself or others who were battling to get their luggage.

Frustration was building as people pushed and jiggled to get out of the airport and off to wherever they were heading. The final stage of entrance to Ecuador was handing over the papeles blancos (white papers) to a dazed looking official who wasn't interested in why I had ticked a box on the paper. People behind me weren't too happy at my attempts to explain either, so having done my best I heaved my case on to the belt followed by my cabin baggage and handbag, and before I knew it, the doors were opening to let me out into the next stage of this adventure. And what better way for it to begin than to look up and see Samuel walking towards me with a huge grin, arms open, and a gorgeous bunch of yellow roses.

My first day in Ecuador was a time to rest and think about why God had taken me there. I spent time with Cecilia, Samuel's other grandmother, and we talked about what was happening in their lives, with Fernando Sr. fighting lung cancer and the impact of this on the family. We talked about faith and religion and God the Healer. Cecilia allowed me to pray for her, for respite from the constant pain in her hip and leg. She was surprised and happy when the pain went. The next day she told me she had the best sleep for a long while. Cecilia is a reiki practitioner and has a special room at the back of the house where people come to her for treatment. I wasn't sure how to talk to her about reiki and divine healing as she sees reiki as being God at work. While this didn't seem to be a battle I needed to engage in, there was something not quite right. I did not feel welcome, and at times there was a sense of danger. I felt fearful and anxious and especially at night, I really struggled. As I prayed and asked for wisdom and discernment in this, I knew that whether or not I wanted to be, I was in a battle. The spirit of reiki did not want me in the house. Prior to this I knew about reiki but had never encountered someone who practised it or had anything to do with it in a practical sense. So, while I knew I could not raise this with Cecilia, I also knew I had to draw some boundaries. This was where Holy Spirit gave me wisdom to pray and spiritually fence off my room. I had no authority in the rest of the house, but I did have authority over my room and what could enter. Also, once I recognised what was happening, I took authority in Jesus' name over this spirit so that it could not make my life difficult anymore. The following verses came alive for me during that time, and I understood them so much better for seeing them at work: *"For though we walk (live) in the flesh, we are not carrying on our warfare according to the flesh and using mere human weapons.* ⁴ *For the weapons of our warfare are not physical [weapons of flesh and blood], but they are mighty before God for the overthrow and destruction of strongholds,* ⁵ *[Inasmuch as we] refute arguments and theories and reasonings and every proud and lofty thing that sets itself up against the [true] knowledge of God; and we lead every thought and purpose away captive into the obedience of Christ (the Messiah, the Anointed One)"* (2 Corinthians 10:3-6).

After a couple of days, the planning me kicked in again, but this time I didn't sense I shouldn't plan. I contacted a couple of people and arranged to see them later in the week. Klaudia Wolff was happy to hear from me and we arranged for me to go to Shell with her and Eckehart the next weekend. I had thought to go for a couple of days, but again, God had other plans. Since returning from Ecuador, God has been teaching me what the following verse really means: *"Roll your works upon the Lord [commit and trust them wholly to Him; He will cause your thoughts to become agreeable to His will, and] so shall your plans be established and succeed"* (Proverbs 16:3).

I am getting better at doing this—at rolling all my plans and thoughts onto God (I still like to plan!)—and as I write I laugh and think how much easier it would have been if I'd known this back then.

Later that first week, I travelled from the Valley up to Quito to meet long-time friends Ruth Ann and Elsi for lunch. Hernan, who became my chofer (taxi driver), dropped me outside HCJB, and we arranged a time for him to be back there to meet me. Hernan, who was always reliable and never kept me waiting, became a special friend while I was there—we spent a lot of time together as he drove me back and forth to Quito and had some great conversations. He allowed me to share my story with him and to share Jesus with him, too. In fact, sharing Jesus was something that just came naturally while I was in Ecuador. People were open and wanted to hear why I was there and what I was doing. So, I told them. If I was open and in tune with Holy Spirit, every meeting with someone was an opportunity.

One evening, I was on my way to the HCJB complex from Ruth Ann and Elsi's apartment, as I was to speak to a group of ladies about what God had been doing since we left Ecuador. My taxi driver was from Quito; Hernan lived in the Valley, and it would have been too far for him to travel to take me such a short distance. The trip was about fifteen minutes, and in that time, God touched Roberto's life. Roberto was Ecuadorian and, like many of his countrymen, had moved to Spain to have a better life. He and his wife started a restaurant there. With the economic crisis in Europe, Roberto had returned to Ecuador to see if things might be better in his home country. He left his wife and two children in Spain while he tested the waters. He was unhappy, as it wasn't working out as he had hoped, and he didn't know what to do. I told him about Ileana and Sarah and some more of our story and prayed for him. He was very moved and told me he had prayed and asked God to show him what he should do. He believed our meeting was a divine appointment, that through it God had confirmed to him that he should go back to Spain and be with his family. Meetings like this one happened all the time I was in Ecuador, and each time I just had to open my mouth and trust Holy Spirit that the right words would come out—not only the right words in the sense of the intention but also the right words in Spanish. Sometimes it was a long way round to get a brief message across, but those times were blessed, and brought a lightness to the moment.

Right from the very beginning I saw differences as I looked back to when we were there before. What made the difference was my relationship with God. This time it was real, and I was constantly aware of Holy Spirit's presence, a presence that was evident in conversations that flowed with words of wisdom and knowledge that surprised me as much as the person I spoke them to—like Roberto. I knew I was there for a limited time and that, even though I didn't have a plan, God did. So, I tried to be flexible and go with the flow. For me, it was a new level of trusting God and seeing Him work, touching people's lives. All those He brought to me for counselling and prayer received emotional and spiritual healing and sometimes He healed them physically too. And in all of this, something that never ceased to amaze me was that many of those He brought to me for ministry and counselling did not speak English and that meant that I needed to minister and counsel in Spanish–a language I had spoken little over the years. I facilitated writing workshops in Spanish and English. The language could have been a huge stumbling block for me. It was one thing to speak Spanish in a conversational context, but to do it on a professional level was something else. Many people said it was just remembering from when we were there before, but that wasn't the case. The language of counselling and prayer ministry had never been a part of my Spanish vocabulary, so for all intents and purposes, it was the equivalent of God giving me another spiritual language. While I was in Shell, Klaudia, a medical doctor and counsellor who has a monthly radio program that goes out to most of Pastaza Province and perhaps even farther, asked me to be her guest on the program. She was to interview me about depression and anxiety, what it is like to experience these illnesses, and how God can help us overcome them. Again, I could share from experience—my own and as a counsellor working with those who suffer from these illnesses—in Spanish! Later, just before leaving Ecuador, I was interviewed about grief for radio, and they also videoed the interview to be used for training for people studying to be counsellors. So as far as language is concerned, God constantly stretched me—I think to show me that I could trust Him, even in this. Part of my ability to trust was in believing that God would only bring people to me that He wanted me to have time with, and so, in believing this, I also believed He would equip me or had equipped me to do whatever I needed to do at the time.

There was a constant flow of people to see and minister to while I was in Ecuador. If I had any thoughts before I went that I might have a holiday or that I would be sitting around, they were quickly put to rest. While in Shell, where I ended up staying for a week, and could have remained longer, I saw several people, both missionary and local. And each one of them said they had been praying for someone to come who could help them. God used that time and the experiences he has taken me through to minister to all those who came. But not only that, God, through me, showed each one that He heard them, and He cared. As they shared this with me, I could see a new level of awareness in them of God's goodness and kindness, a deepening of relationship with Him. It awed them that God would do this. Each time I saw someone, each time they trusted me enough to share with me their deepest hurts and concerns, I found that God had prepared me in advance with experiences in my own life that gave me the ability to empathise with them, to know what they were struggling with in a way that went far beyond being a counsellor. This was so in Quito as well.

Mery and Gonzalo Reyes had become special friends when we lived in Shell, so I was excited when Florence Judd, an Australian missionary, now retired, who spent many years in Shell, said she would take me over to visit them. They weren't expecting me, and I wondered if they would even remember me. Gonzalo was home working in his workshop and as we approached, I called his name, *"Gonzalo."* He looked up and didn't even hesitate, calling, *"Señora Karen!"* as he rushed to hug me. Mery, who works for Compassion International at one of the Projects located close to Puyo, was not far away, he said, and even as we were talking, he noticed her coming along the street. I turned to see for myself and Mery's response was as instantaneous as Gonzalo's. What a reunion that was. After so many years, to be together again was very special. Florence left me with them, as I thought I could find my way back to the compound. But, as it happened, I didn't need to. Gonzalo pulled out his mobile phone and called all the children. Some I had never met (I found that Mery and Gonzalo had named two of their daughters after me and Miriam), and others I remembered as toddlers. All those who could come, did.

What a joy it was to meet Jessica again, and not only that, but to meet her daughter, Aslint. Jessica and our Sarah had really hit it off; they were about the same age when they met, and it was good to reminisce about times we had together without feeling we couldn't mention the girls. Soon that visit was over, but not before Gonzalo gave me some of their eggs—blue, green, and yellow shells! We laughed about that and compared stories of Australian and Ecuadorian chooks. Jessica and Aslint walked me back, just to make sure I got there safely. I thought of Sarah and what it would have been like if she were there with us, and Jessica and I talked about that openly and shed a few tears together.

We had another few hours together before I travelled back to Quito, and they made my time with them special. Knowing my concern about travelling back to Quito on a bus, Jessica even offered to travel with me. They are so giving, so selfless, and it blessed me to have that time with them.

When I returned to Quito, I knew I was to share at a meeting that Denise, the Personnel Director of HCJB, had arranged. We had talked about it before I went to Shell, and she contacted me while there to tell me that it was all organised and, as so many missionaries were on HMA, she had no idea how many would be there. We were to have a potluck meal and then I would speak. I remember saying to her that it didn't matter how many came; we would just trust God to bring the ones He wanted there. It was a good mix of people from various missions and from the British and US Embassies, about twenty-two in all. It was a powerful evening and out of it came a couple of weeks of individual counselling and prayer ministry. Ruth Ann and Elsi allowed me to use a room in the Centre for Christian Communication (CCC) building. Ruth Ann and Elsi opened their hearts and their home to me, and it was as though I was family to them. We chatted and laughed and cried a bit too, sharing deep things easily and praying together spontaneously in a way that was remarkable considering we hadn't seen each other for so many years, and had rarely been in touch during that time.

It was interesting the way things opened up after that meeting so that I spent more time in Quito than I did in the Valley. Once people knew I was there and I was happy to see anyone who felt they needed help, I had a constant flow of people coming. I also facilitated a couple of writing workshops with a powerful effect for those who took part, and I had a morning in Atahualpa Women's Prison. One of the prisoners, a young American woman, stood out to me. She was there as many were because they had been caught being drug couriers. I asked her why she had done it, particularly since she was pregnant and also had a small child back home in the States. Her response was that it was worth the risk because if she hadn't been caught, the money would have made a big difference in her life. We talked about

God, and she was convinced God wouldn't want anything to do with her because of the poor choices she had made. Wow! That sounded familiar. The enemy certainly is not creative in the lies he spins. Sadly, though, he is effective until the lies are revealed for what they are. I had a strong desire to pray for the young woman that day and a strong sense that Father God was reaching out, through those of us who were there, to touch her. I was hoping she would have that aha moment then and there. She looked at me when I finished praying and said, *"Thank you, those words touched my heart."* I don't know where the young woman is now, but I know God is at work, and I know that one day that young woman will walk into His waiting arms.

I could never have imagined doing all that I did while I was in Ecuador. If I had planned, I would have limited God. As it was, each day was a new day, and each day there was someone new for me to see. In many ways, the purpose of my planning would have been to protect me; there was still something in me that feared rejection, feared not being good enough and not meeting expectations. This could have thrown me back to my old way of responding. The fear of rejection can compel us to become the person we believe others will recognise or accept, which will vary to some degree with each new group or situation. And with each change we make to comply with external circumstances, there is a subtle erosion of the consistency and stability of our personality. Soon we are confused about who we really are and therefore can be controlled almost completely by external circumstances. That's why the Bible tells us not to be double minded, hesitant, doubting, or uncertain, rather to be strong and resolute. Confidence in who we are as children of God, loved and rescued by Him, is significant. But this means being separated from all we have known and been so that He can make us into the person He created us to be. He calls us to live by faith in Him alone and not to rely on our own understanding. What a challenge! I saw this happening in Ecuador this time—relying on Him, trusting rather than planning.

Looking Back Moving Forward - Return to Ecuador

The day I returned to our old apartment building was bittersweet. Samuel was with me, and I am so glad he was. He was a great support. Manuel was still there and looking just the same. He and Ileana had a special relationship.

We walked up the front steps. I pointed out the window to our bedroom on the first floor and told the story of the night the bullet came through, fired by someone in an altercation outside the night club that was across the road. I told Samuel how his mother sneaked out by letting herself down over the balcony, somehow doing it without breaking any bones, and more importantly, without us hearing her! And all the time as I recalled stories, as I told Samuel what it was like, I could feel my breathing becoming more difficult, my eyes filling with tears. Then he hugged me a little tighter. *"It's OK Grandma,"* he said. I took a deep breath as we entered the lift that took us to Cecilia's apartment on the top floor of the building. Cecilia is the landlady, an aristocratic lady with Spanish ancestry evident in her features, strong and determined, a very good businesswoman. As we were leaving, she hugged me—unusual for Cecilia, and she told Samuel he was welcome there anytime and if he ever needed help while in Quito he was to call—a gracious lady. After our visit with Cecilia, it was easy to slip back into conversation with Manuel; it was as though the years had never passed. We spent a little time together until he was called away to one of his many tasks. He insisted I had to return, but next time I was to make sure Señor Ross was with me.

I didn't think I needed to return to Ecuador. Whenever someone asked if we would go back, I always shrugged and said, *"No. There's no need. That part of our life is over."* I think I still believed that when God told me it was time to return to Ecuador. It wasn't until I was there, and the days began to pass with God bringing people and situations that were both challenging and blessing that I could see that perhaps I needed to go back. At some point, and I can't say exactly when, awareness dawned that I held Ecuador responsible for the deaths of Ileana and Sarah; I held it against Ecuador and the people of Ecuador. How like God to take me back and to allow me to work with Him to bring healing and wholeness to some I considered my enemies because of what had happened to our children. As I ministered, I was ministered to, and so forgiveness and healing became intertwined, and at a subconscious level, I opened my heart and let the anger, the resentment, and the disdain go. Just a few days before I left, someone asked me to see a lady who was struggling with grief. It was on this day I heard Holy Spirit whisper to me, *"You are bringing healing and hope in a place where you lost hope, where you were wounded so badly, and in turn you are finally healed. Rejoice!"*

Maria is a lovely Quichua lady whose four-year-old daughter was diagnosed with leukaemia. In February 2012, the little girl was admitted to hospital again for tests and treatment and Maria was told she would be perfectly all right and would not need to go back to hospital for five years. Just a few days later, the little one died. Maria was devastated and by the time I arrived in June, she was struggling so badly that my friend Kathy Jo asked if I would see Maria. I spent a couple of hours with her and there was a strong sense of a supernatural presence as we talked. In such a difficult and memory provoking situation, I saw God at work using all that had happened to me to minister to Maria. It was a real battle, and exhausting, for both of us. This was a story so near to my own in many ways, and for God to use that as my final time of ministry was a powerful way of showing me that the words He spoke to me that afternoon after the workshop, so many years before, had come to pass. *"You can do this; you can use what has happened in your life to help others."*

Looking Back Moving Forward - Return to Ecuador

Try this:

Think about looking back, moving forward, then try the following writing exercise:

1. You are standing at the edge of a narrow bridge with no rails. You want to cross to the other side but are worried about the dangerous drop below you. Describe the bridge, your surroundings, why you want to cross, how you feel.
2. You become aware of a person or people on the far bank. They are calling to you. Write about this and the effect on you.

It is in the stillness that we hear God speak, and stillness is vital if we are to hear the conversation going on in heaven about our life and situation. Try this stillness exercise:

1. Find a comfortable place.
2. Gently close your eyes.
3. Slow your breathing down—take two deep breaths, inhaling deeply and exhaling until it feels as though you can't breathe out anymore.
4. Imagine your mind is a still, quiet pool, and quietly ask Holy Spirit to drop a word into that pool.
5. If you have stray thoughts, acknowledge them, and let them go.
6. Bring your focus back to waiting on God and expect him to speak.

Each time you do this, you train your mind to focus and to be still before the Lord.

GRIEF

In some ways suffering ceases to be suffering at the moment it finds a meaning, such as the meaning of a sacrifice.

— Viktor Frankl

It was November. Again. Every year November turns up. It's a given. And every year, for a long time after Illy and Sarah died, something changed in me at the beginning of November. It was like a switch was flicked; I could have been Dr Jekyll and Mr Hyde. I became irritable, snappy, sleep was minimal, I cried easily, and my mood was all over the place. As the days marched on towards November 20th, my feelings became even more intense.

Anniversary reactions—feeling grief at the same time of year that we initially experience a loss is not something I understood. It took me a while to figure out and understand what was happening to me. In fact, understanding grief was something that took me a long while to do. And perhaps, if I'm totally honest, I don't fully understand it now, so many years after our daughters died.

It's important to acknowledge that grief isn't something we deal with and walk away from. Grief stays with us. It takes different forms as the years pass, and it morphs and changes depending on what is happening in our life, but it's always with us.

It wasn't until I became a therapist that I began to see the many faces of grief. I saw it in those experiencing losses other than the death of a loved one, too. Grief revealed itself to me in clients diagnosed with depression and anxiety who came for help to deal with those illnesses. As we worked together, I would feel the tug of grief. Once I saw it there, it would take a word, or a sentence, not much more, for all that was hiding the grief to unravel and allow it to show itself. And then, of course, God showed me I still had more grieving to do.

It was the anniversary grief that I needed to face first. In Tasmania, November is always a beautiful, light time when leaves on budding trees are almost completely unfurled, baby birds are still in their nests, beaks open waiting for the tasty morsels their parents are foraging for, and there's such a lot of bird-chatter and singing, you can't help but be joyful. Yet, on those sun-filled, blue-sky days, a sadness so deep would overwhelm me and all I wanted to do was weep. I missed my girls. I wanted to hold them. I didn't care that they were safe with God and probably wouldn't want to come back to me. I just wanted to hold them, hug them, and tell them how much I love them.

'Depression.'

I stared at my doctor. 'Seriously? Depression?'

'Well, yes. You have all the symptoms. Even the road rage. The anger. I'll give you a prescription …'

'I don't want a prescription. I'm not taking medication.' I knew I was being difficult. The easiest thing would have been to take the prescription and not have it filled. But I wanted more than this. More than—a prescription. I wanted to talk to someone. I knew it was unreasonable to think my doctor could be that person. She was already behind and still had a line of people waiting to see her.

'Well, you could see a psychologist.' She peered over her glasses and handed me the prescription. 'Take this anyway,' she smiled, 'just in case.'

Being my usual stubborn self, I decided to do some research. I had an inkling that what was wrong with me had something to do with grief. I had avoided it for a long time. Yet, even as I avoided facing my own grief, God was sending me clients whom I was helping to be brave, to face *their* grief, to work through it, and with it, to move forward in life after devastating losses. I sat in the car for a while after leaving the surgery and debated whether I should just get the prescription filled or whether this was God's way of telling me it was time for me to stop running. If that were the case, I knew how hard it could be. Perhaps it was time for me to be as brave as my clients were.

After I turned back to God and had such an amazing experience of restoration and a power encounter with Holy Spirit, I assumed everything was done; that I would be OK and God would take away all the pain, the sorrow, the heartache, and from then on, life would be, if not easy, then certainly without too much upheaval. After all, we'd had our share of all the hard stuff, so surely there wouldn't be any more.

In many ways, the turning back was just the beginning. Being right with God did not give me a ticket out of life's challenges. It gave me the confidence, though, that God would be with me in those challenges, and He would see me through them. In choosing to go towards the pain of grief, I was putting my newfound trust in God to the test. I can't say I didn't have doubts that He would be there for me. My mind often raced back to what God said when I was uncertain and afraid before we went to Ecuador.

'I will be with you.'

'But last time. What if—' And as quickly as those words flashed across my mind, others followed, 'No turning back …'

Trust in the Lord with all of your heart, I muttered to myself as I decided to lean into the grief, to stop running from it.

It was then I read an article about anniversary grief.

Journalling is a way I process things. When I turned to my journal, I found I could trace my November reactions back to after the girls died. I read the entries for each year, and it was clear what was happening.

As soon as the calendar clicked over to November, the mood changes, irritability, and other reactions set in. Once I understood I was experiencing an anniversary reaction—that I was mourning, not depressed, it was so much easier to talk about what was happening. It was helpful for Ross too, to know that what I was experiencing was normal, a normal response to grief. And it also helped me to work better with my clients. Those Novembers for many years were times of re-experiencing the grief of a monumental loss, and it was OK. I wasn't weak or even stuck in my grief. I was mourning the loss of my two precious daughters.

Recently, in another November, God showed me yet another aspect of grief I needed to face. Out of that came a new book, A Grief Revealed. It's a book of stories; stories about grief that often goes unacknowledged by others, especially those close to us, and it's about a lost possible self. In that recent November my anniversary grief took the form of mourning the loss of me as a mother and grandmother to Illy and Sarah and their children—a grief I hadn't fully understood until I began writing the book.

As I've journeyed with grief, I've found it helpful to consider grief as a person. A person whose mission isn't to harm me, but to work with God to teach me and continue to nudge me in the direction I need to go. My eyes have been opened to see grief in places I never would have before. Sometimes it hovers around the edges, no more than a miasma, while at other times it is almost overpowering. Below is a poem I wrote about grief as the person it was to me at various times over the past years:

> Grief comes with heavy footsteps
>
> Slow, inevitable, heavy footsteps.
>
> It does not stop, no matter what the barrier.
>
> It marks time,
> Pounding in place,
> Waiting ...
>
> Grief knows it cannot be stopped.

Grief

I turn to face it and
The power of it overwhelms

I drop
The pain sharp and fierce

And Grief speaks

"Look at me."

I refuse
Obstinate, hateful thing you are

How can you demand this of me?

How?

"Look at me."

It isn't a request.
I look
And in the face of Grief
I see everything that is in me

Everything.

And the tears break through the dammed wall,

The pain finds voice shrieking in protest.

Every part of me tries to draw back but

It's too late.

I sob, I shout, I rant,

I hurt, hurt, hurt

And all the while Grief remains

Steadfast
Until the tears stop, the pain subsides.

"Now then," says Grief, "let's do the real work."

Looking Back Moving Forward

Grief doesn't always show up as it does above. Sometimes it is a quiet presence, a gentle press of a hand on my shoulder, a whisper of encouragement to allow the sadness, the tears—for a while. And then I hear God's voice speaking through Grief, reminding me that He is with me, that He loves me, and this is simply another part of the journey. If Grief is to do its work, we need to allow it to. Our job is, as I mentioned earlier, to lean into it. I've learned that when I am in God's hands, I can come out the other side of wherever Grief takes me, and I can come out stronger.

Try this:

Sometimes grief seems like a companion on our journey. If grief were a person, what would he or she be like? Write, or draw, how you see grief in your life at this moment.

Loss is a part of life. Some losses are harder to bear than others. What is the loss that you are grieving now? What do you need so that you grieve well for this loss?

AFTERWORD

One of the most important lessons I have learned is that my past and present do not determine my future. Yes, God has done amazing things in my life, but He is not finished yet. All that I have shared in this book brings us to the present moment, but there is more. The old me would have lived in fear, constantly wondering what terrible things might happen, trying to control everything to make sure I, and those I care about, were safe, or bemoaning not having all I felt I needed to be happy!

My personality was a mess for several reasons. Because of this, I built walls around myself, defenses to keep people, and God, from hurting me. I was locking others out, but I was also locking myself in. Being so filled with fear, I became a controller, as this was the only way I could keep myself safe.

Jesus came to open prison doors and set the captives free. I didn't make any progress until I believed I could be free. I had to have a positive vision for my life, which included a God who loves me and will never harm me; I had to believe that my future was not determined by my past, nor even my present.

You may have had a horrible past; your present circumstances may be negative and depressing. In fact, what you are facing now may be so awful it seems there is no hope. Don't believe it. That is a lie. In God, there is always hope. He showed me that, and He will show you too.

Changing our mindset and renewing our minds means seeing God as He really is, changing our view or image of Him. Ask God to show you what mindsets need to change and be willing to work with Him as He reveals to you who He really is. As I work with my heavenly Father rather than against Him, I continue to grow in the knowledge of His loving care, and in faith, conviction, and courage. I encourage you to take the time to quietly, and in trusting confidence, get to know the One who loves you perfectly. And as you do, consider the following verse that St. Paul offers us as encouragement:

> Keep putting into practice all you learned from me—everything you heard from me and saw me doing. Then the God of peace will be with you.
> — **Philippians 4:9 (NLT)**

ALSO BY KAREN

If you have found this book helpful, you might also find Karen's recently published *A Grief Revealed*, helpful. Read on for a taste of what you will find in *A Grief Revealed*.

INTRODUCTION

My friend, Julie, and I were sitting at a cafe having lunch. Earlier in the year, we had committed to meeting together once a month to write. It was to keep us accountable, we said. So, there we were, meeting and eating and talking, not doing too much writing, but talking about writing and our work. I'm a counsellor, and I had been mulling over what I really wanted to specialise in as I was tired of trying to be all things to all people.

'I don't know what my thing is.'

'You don't know?' Julie chuckled, raising her eyebrows as she peered at me with a *'seriously?'* look on her face. 'I do.'

'You do?' I was surprised. 'What is it? What's my thing, then?'

'Grief. Grief's your thing.' There was certainty in her voice, and the way she sat back in her chair after making the declaration showed me she wasn't expecting an argument.

'Really? Grief?'

I pondered it for a bit, thinking back to the stories I had written, the novel I was working on and the expressive writing workshops I loved to run. Grief was a common thread running through them all: loss, pain, sadness, resilience and overcoming; a walking through and with; sometimes alone, sometimes with others. I had to agree. Grief was—and still is—my thing.

Writing is my thing too, as is storytelling.

I didn't set out to write a book about grief. I was already busy working on a novel and working with my clients, so beginning another project went against all I was trying to do—reduce stress by reducing my workload! Then November came around. The anniversary of the death of my daughters, Sarah and Ileana, was upon us again. It's been almost thirty years since that horrific day in November 1993 when my world was turned upside down and pain like I had never experienced before bit into the very heart of me. Despite the passage of time some years continue to be harder than others and, for some reason—I still don't understand why—November 2020 was especially hard. Perhaps because COVID-19 hit the world in 2020 and I saw the lives of many others turned upside down; perhaps something in me resonated with that. Whatever the reason, I noticed the grief that people weren't even aware they were carrying. Sometimes it hid behind depression or anxiety; sometimes it masked itself as frustration or anger or disappointment. Yet, if I prodded just a little, scratched the surface a tiny bit, the grief began to leak out.

The kind of grief I was seeing was what psychology calls disenfranchised grief. One writer, Thomas Attig, suggests the nature of this disenfranchisement is denial of the mourner's 'right to grieve'. Once settled with the idea that grief was my thing, I had no plans to do more than work with that, to continue doing what I had always done when I worked with clients—help them find what was behind their current pain, help them see it was OK to grieve. But, in November, the month our daughters died so many years ago, I decided I wanted to write about grief. At first it was to be a retelling of my story and my relationship with grief—and just for me. Because in the retelling of my life story, I knew I could change the way I related to my circumstances, to what had happened to me that had caused me to see myself as a victim for so long. I knew the power of my story and decided it was time to write another chapter of it.

Introduction

Then, as I considered those I worked with, considered the pain they suffered and their attempts to hide it, as I reflected on each of their stories, I knew I wanted to write about their experiences of grief too. Many of them hadn't realised that what they were experiencing was grief because they associated grief with death and dying. I saw the bewilderment on their faces when I said to them, 'You're grieving.'

One young woman was quick to respond when I suggested she might not be depressed, but rather that she was deep in a state of grief.

'My doctor said I am depressed, and he's prescribed an antidepressant. Here,' she rummaged in her bag and pulled out a small box neatly labelled with her name and the details of the medication, 'I must be depressed.' She insisted I take it and note down what the doctor prescribed, frowning at me and biting her lip as I did. 'Why would I be grieving?'

'Tell me your story again,' I urged.

And as her story tumbled out, the tears fell. So much loss. Loss upon loss upon loss.

When C.S. Lewis's wife died, he told of how his grief was deep and overwhelming. He said, 'No one ever told me grief was like fear. I am not afraid, but the sensation is like being afraid.' The young woman recently diagnosed with depression told me of her deep fear that she wouldn't ever get past what had happened to her, that she would never be a wife or a mother because no one would want her if they knew how unworthy she was.

'Sometimes the fear is too much. I can't bear it.' She wrapped her arms around her middle and rocked a little.

There are several definitions of grief, but essentially it is a feeling of intense sorrow and sadness, the mental and emotional suffering and distress caused by loss and regret. By the end of our time together, the young woman acknowledged that she was grieving and agreed to work with me to find and navigate her path through the huge losses she had experienced.

Looking Back Moving Forward

Walking the path is not quick, and it's rarely easy. In fact, sometimes it feels like you need a machete to slash your way through; sometimes it's like you are walking through thick mud that wants to suck you down and it's all you can do to lift one foot at a time to take a step forward. I suggested to a lovely young lady that the path might, at times, seem a bit like navigating the fire swamp seen in the iconic movie, *A Princess Bride*. Although there are many dangers and obstacles on her path, she has someone who is journeying with her and helping her when she feels unable to help herself, or when she cannot see the danger. Even so, she still has to get through the swamp! She laughed and decided she would go home and watch the movie again.

'That's just what it feels like, but, yes, you're right. I'm not in this alone. Thanks for reminding me of that.'

This came from another young woman who didn't believe she had a valid reason to grieve. Because no one had died, and because she believed she had made bad choices, she blamed herself for where she now found herself. Blamed herself that a person whom she had hoped would love and cherish her had instead turned on her, abused and belittled her. When we talked about the lost possible self, the wife and mother in a safe, caring relationship that she had hoped for and dreamed of, tears dripped slowly onto her jeans-clad lap.

The grief work will be ongoing now that she has given herself permission to grieve. She will learn, as you will as you read this book, that grieving is not just about suffering. Through 'listening' to the stories I tell and doing the writing exercises I have suggested, if you choose to, you will learn that it is possible to experience devastation and suffering, yet reach through them to find hope, and in so doing, affirm life and a sense of purpose that pulls you through. Grieving is about both suffering and resilience. The stories you just read are what it's like for someone stuck in what we call 'disenfranchised grief'. Disenfranchised grief—the denial of a mourner's right to grieve—more than any other kind of grief attempts to bed the griever down in their suffering. They are also about a lost possible self, the loss of

Introduction

dreams and hopes that will never be realised. Throughout the book you will be provided with tools to help you navigate your own path through loss, as you face the grief in your life, or you can use them to help someone you know who is suffering right now. Because writing has been a powerful healing tool for me and for so many I have worked with, I have included an entire section about how writing works, along with several prompts you can use if you choose to allow writing to help you heal.

This book is not an academic treatment of grief. I'd like it to be a conversation with you. When I walk around the lovely, leafy village where I live, I often have conversations going on in my head, and with other people if they happen to be walking when I am. There's one person I walk with when we can manage to be out at the same time, and we often discuss the things I write about in this book. So, I'm inviting you to join the conversation. If you would like to add to it, feel free to do so by leaving a comment on my website: karenmace.com.

I am very grateful to those friends who have generously, and without hesitation, contributed their stories. They have made this a labour of love. I have changed the names and other details to ensure confidentiality except where I have been given express permission to use their first names, and all vignettes are composites of various individuals. Where grief is personified, some see it as he and some as she. I have not changed it to make it one or the other throughout the book as I believe it is important to honour how the writer perceives the personified Grief.

CHAPTER SEVEN

AMELIA

The Box

I see it in my mind's eye. It follows me everywhere, never letting me stray far. I feel it behind me now. If I turn around, I know it will be there, waiting to see if I will pay it some attention. Mostly I don't, but I have come to accept that it will always be there.

What follows me is a little box, tied with a bow. It looks very much like it contains a gift or a treasure, but I know it doesn't. Even though it's mine, I don't really want it. I often wonder, *does everyone have a little box like this?*

I'm no longer afraid to pick it up, to look at it and examine its edges. Sometimes I even undo the bow and take a peek inside—but only if I have to. I'd rather not pick it up at all unless absolutely necessary. But I know it is good for me to do this occasionally. And somehow, this practice seems to stop the box from getting bigger than it should. I tried actively ignoring it for a while but discovered that strategy just makes it grow. Then, when I'm not looking, and at often the most inopportune time, it explodes. Much like a jack-in-the-box. The contents are strewn everywhere for all to see. It takes time to gather the items and put them back in.

The weight of the box is surprising given its size. The contents vary, although two items remain constants: a blank piece of paper and a coin.

The blank piece of paper

On this paper I write the current form my grief is taking: the longing for more children; the pain of being around new babies; grief that my husband has never really seemed to understand at all (it bewilders him), and the loneliness I feel; and a variety of other narratives, mostly self-indulgent and entirely unhelpful but they need to be expressed nonetheless—otherwise they grow bigger. Somehow, by writing them on this (imaginary) blank piece of paper and putting them in the box, they lose their power, and I am able to move on. The next time I open the box, the paper is blank again.

I struggle to name a specific experience of grief because I find it so pervasive and it surprises me by popping up everywhere, often when I least expect it. The lost possible self is a constant theme: the 'me' who imagined I would have the career, while hubby would be the house husband (because that's what he said he wanted all those years ago). We would have four children and life would be peachy. But instead, my inner voice says: *give up your training and follow him overseas because his dream is to re-train* (he would've gone with or without me); *oh, and then give it all up again* (the new career I had carved from scratch) *because he now wants to move back home; and here, now run this business. Sure, you can keep practising as long as you keep doing the other stuff, running the house, running the business ... and don't worry about that miscarriage ... what do you mean you want more children? Let's not do more children, let's do breast cancer instead. But don't worry, your friend nearby will keep on popping out babies, so at least you'll be close to babies all the time.*

As you can see, it's messy.

The coin

The coin is marked with a word written in tiny print on the outside edge: longing. On each side is a different word: 'hope' on one side, 'regret' on the other. I know what they mean. Hope looks forward and points to the possibility that something is yet to be: that the story is not yet over, and the final chapter will tie all things together, so it makes sense.

On the other side, 'regret' looks backwards and reflects those things that might have been, the discordance between the 'dreamed-for' and the actual reality. It encompasses the things I wish I'd done, or think may've changed the situation that is my current reality. It comes with a hefty dose of guilt for the role I've played in the status quo. I know that 'regret' is the danger side, because there is an underlying 'if only' assumption that has a God-like quality to it:

'If I were God, I would've written a different script.'

I guess both sides of the coin point to a kind of bargaining that I still engage in. As I think about them, even now, there is a lump in my throat. But I am always eventually drawn back to the 'hope' side. Maybe, just maybe, God can make good this mess.

Romans 8:28 says that for those who love him, God causes all things to work together for good.

ACKNOWLEDGEMENTS

So many people to thank ...

Claire van Ryn has been a huge support and encouragement as I've worked on this revision. I'm grateful for her input, her willingness to read and give feedback, and the shoring up of my sometimes-waning confidence. Most of all I am grateful for her godly wisdom and prayers. Julie Sladden, writing partner extraordinaire, let's continue to encourage each other! Denise and Sarah, I'm so thankful for your great proofreading, and to the Ultimate 48 Hour author team for their support.

I am grateful for my good friends who have supported me as I've worked on this project, and especially those in our small connect group who have prayed for me. Ross, thank you for always being there for me and for knowing when to pull me away from my books and computer for a break, and Miriam, my beautiful daughter and friend thank you for reading everything I write and telling me it is wonderful!

ABOUT THE AUTHOR

Karen A Mace is the author of Healing Begins in the Heart, A Grief Revealed and the companion workbooks. She is a registered counsellor and writing therapist with academic degrees in counselling, nursing, education, and psychology, and brings elements of all of these to her writing as well as her Christian faith which is foundational to her work. Karen has completed two works of fiction, which she hopes to launch into the world in the coming months. She and her husband live in beautiful Tasmania, in a location perfect for writing.

You can connect with Karen online at karenmace.com and chat with her on Instagram at @karenmacewriter or on Facebook at @karenmacewriter.

KAREN A MACE

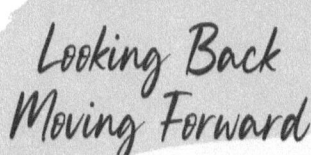

Looking Back Moving Forward

Other Publications by Karen

> Graceful. Intimate. Intelligent. An unfolding of sunlight and hope. For anyone touched by the edges of grief, or unravelling from its centre, Karen A. Mace's "A Grief Revealed" is a touchstone for finding one's way back into joy and wholeness.
> Tammy

> Thank you so much for writing the book. As soon as I read the first chapter, I knew it was for me. It's opened up things I didn't realise were there. I'm very grateful because it's helping me to make sense of a lot of things.
> Wendy

> I just finished your book and everything I read applies to me. I know I need to grieve but I haven't known how. This book has given me the courage to ask for help.
> Dani

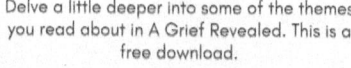

Delve a little deeper into some of the themes you read about in A Grief Revealed. This is a free download.

Healing Begins in the Heart, the first edition of Looking Back Moving Forward.

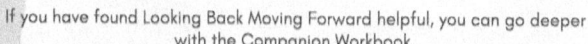

If you have found Looking Back Moving Forward helpful, you can go deeper with the Companion Workbook.
This Workbook is for you if you want to explore, in more depth, the themes that are present in Looking Back Moving Forward. It will work equally well for you if you want to work alone with God on what He has shown you as you have read the book, as it will if you want to go deeper into those themes with a small group.
A Grief Revealed available from Amazon, Book Depository and all good book stores and from **karenmace.com**

Healing Begins in the Heart available only from **karenmace.com**
Workbooks are available for download only from **karenmace.com**

NOTES

www.ingramcontent.com/pod-product-compliance
Lightning Source LLC
Chambersburg PA
CBHW021152080526
44588CB00008B/308